My plea for
the Old Sword

My plea for
the Old Sword

THE UNSURPASSABLE PRE-EMINENCY OF THE ENGLISH
AUTHORIZED VERSION (KJV) OF THE HOLY BIBLE

IAN R. K. PAISLEY

AMBASSADOR
Belfast • Greenville

My plea for *the Old Sword*

Copyright © 1997 Ian R. K. Paisley

All rights reserved
No part of this book may be reproduced, stored in a retrieval system,
or transmitted in any form or by any means - electronic, mechanical,
photocopy, recording or otherwise - without written permission of the
publisher, except for brief quotations in printed reviews.

ISBN 1 84030 015 9

AMBASSADOR PRODUCTIONS LTD,
Providence House
16 Hillview Avenue,
Belfast, BT5 6JR
Northern Ireland

Emerald House,
1 Chick Springs Road, Suite 206
Greenville,
South Carolina 29609
United States of America

Foreword

A great educationalist, Mr. J. Paton once said, *"If men read trash they think trash and if they think trash they become trash."*

The opposite is, of course, also true. If men read God's truth they think God's truth and if they think God's truth they become true.

"Ye shall know the truth," said our Lord Jesus Christ, *"and the truth shall set you free."*

The Bible is pure as the naked heavens, majestic, free.

"Take up and read" is the divine command to everyone.

When other helps and comforts flee the Bible is a very present help in trouble. It remaineth.

A book is the measure of the inner life of its author, and in the Bible we have revealed to us the mystery of the inner life of the Triune Jehovah God, the One True God of Israel.

How better could I end this foreword than with this extract from the preface to the Authorised Version.

"It remaineth that we commend thee [gentle reader] to God and to the Spirit of His Grace, which is able to build further than we can ask or think. He removeth the scales from our eyes, the vail from our hearts, opening our wits that we may understand His word, enlarging our hearts, yea correcting our affections, that we may love it above gold and silver, yea that we may love it to the end. Ye are brought unto fountains of living water which ye digged not; do not cast earth into them with the Philistines, neither prefer broken pits before them with the wicked Jews. Others have laboured, and you may enter into their labours. O receive not so great things in vain: O despise not so great salvation ... It is a fearful thing to fall into the hands of the living God; but a blessed thing it is and will bring us to everlasting blessedness in the end, when God speaketh to us, to hearken; when He setteth His word before us, to read it; when He stretcheth out His hand and calleth, to answer, here am I, here we are to do Thy will, O God. The Lord work a care and conscience in us to know Him and serve Him, that we may be acknowledged of Him at the appearing of our Lord Jesus Christ, to whom with the Holy Ghost, be all praise and thanksgiving, Amen."

Ian R. K. Paisley
Eph 6:19 + 20

IAN R. K. PAISLEY
October 1997

Martyrs Memorial Chruch
356-376 Ravenhill Road,
Belfast,
BT6 8GL
Northern Ireland
United Kingdom

Contents

Introduction 9

1 **The foundation of the English Authorised Version (KJV) of the Holy Bible is unsurpassably pre-eminent in** *the underlying texts upon which it rests*............................ 13

2 **The foundation of the English Authorised Version (KJV) of the Holy Bible is unsurpassably pre-eminent in** *the various English versions which gave it birth and of which it is the sum and substance, the pith and marrow, the essence, cream and perfection* 24

3 **The translators of the English Authorised Version (KJV) of the Holy Bible are pre-eminent in** *their saintliness and scholarship, the providential way they were so singularly brought together, and the dedication with which they undertook and gloriously completed their mammoth task* 30

4 **The translation of the English Authorised Version (KJV) of the Holy Bible is unsurpassably pre-eminent in** *the techniques it employed* 40

5 The language of the English Authorised Version (KJV) of the Holy Bible is unsurpassably pre-eminent
being the first from the well undefiled and indeed the very well itself 49

6 The foundation of the English Authorised Version (KJV) of the Holy Bible is unsurpassably pre-eminent in
majesty, chastity and eternity 59

7 The doctrine of the English Authorised Version (KJV) of the Holy Bible is unsurpassably pre-eminent
being couched in sound words in keeping with unwavering belief in the revealed truths of the Word of God 73

8 The reverence of the English Authorised Version (KJV) of the Holy Bible is unsurpassably pre-eminent
casting the hem of its holy garment over every sentence, word and syllable 93

9 The history of the English Authorised Version (KJV) of the Holy Bible is unsurpassably pre-eminent,
having preserved for centuries the Word of God for the English speaking peoples of the whole world, and those evangelised by them 101

10 The fruits of the English Authorised Version (KJV) of the Holy Bible are unsurpassably pre-eminent,
being so mighty and so manifold that there is not room enough to receive them 108

Introduction

Let me state quite simply and plainly the position for which I contend.

I believe the Bible is the verbally inspired Word of the living God and because the Authorised Version is a faithful English translation of the original Hebrew of the Old Testament and the original Greek of the New Testament, it is the very Word of God in my mother tongue. Being a translation does not alter one iota of its integrity, inerrancy and infallibility as God's Word.

I believe the Authorised Version preserves the Word of God for me in the English tongue and that it contains no errors.

In the unfolding of its history I trace the providential wonder of the God who both gave His own inerrant Word and transmitted it through many epochs of crucial centuries for the Christian Church

As far as the English Authorized Version is concerned I believe:

1. Its foundation is unsurpassably pre-eminent in the underlying texts upon which it rests.

2. Its ancestry is unsurpassably pre-eminent in the various English translations which gave it birth and of which it is the sum and substance, the pith and marrow, the essence and cream and perfection.

3. Its translators are unsurpassably pre-eminent in their saintliness and scholarship, the way they were providentially brought together, and the dedication with which they undertook and completed their momentous task.

4. Its translation is unsurpassably pre-eminent in the techniques it employed.

5. Its English is unsurpassably pre-eminent.

6. Its language is unsurpassably pre-eminent in its charity, chastity and eternity.

7. Its doctrine is unsurpassably pre-eminent, being couched in sound words, in keeping to the text with unwavering integrity.

8. Its reverence is unsurpassably pre-eminent, casting the hem of its holy garment carefully over every sentence, word and syllable.

9. Its history is unsurpassably pre-eminent, having preserved for centuries the Word of God for the English speaking peoples of the whole world and those evangelised by them.

10. Its fruits are unsurpassably pre-eminent, so mighty and so manifold that there is not room enough to receive them.

I believe this English Authorized Version is unsurpassably pre-eminent over and above all other English translations, because like the blessed Joseph there rests upon it the blessing of the heavens above and of the deep that lieth under (Genesis 49:25).

I cry out "There is none like that, give it me," and in so doing I nail the Satanic lie that the Authorized Version is outdated, outmoded, mistranslated, a relic of the past and only defended by stupid, unlearned, untaught obscurantists.

As its deriders and revilers pass on to the judgment of the thrice holy God whose revelation they despise, the Old Book,

"Incomparable in its faithfulness, majestic in its language, and inexhaustible in its spiritual fruitfulness, continues to reveal to millions the matchless

grace of Him whose name is THE WORD OF GOD, and who is crowned with glory and honour."

I believe this Book will always be the unsurpassable pre-eminent English version of the Holy Bible and no other can ever take its place.

To seek to dislodge this Book from its rightful pre-eminent place is the act of the enemy, and what is attempted to put in its place is an intruder - an imposter - a pretender - a usurper.

Having made my position crystal clear, I will now move to substantiate and defend it.

1 The foundation of the English Authorised Version (KJV) of the Holy Bible is unsurpassably pre-eminent in
the underlying texts upon which it rests

The foundation texts upon which any translation rests are all-important.

If the foundation is false the translation will be false. If the foundation is corrupt the translation will be corrupt. If the foundation is erroneous the translation will be erroneous.

The texts upon which the modern English perversions of the Holy Scripture are founded are neither reliable nor accurate.

Their high claims rest upon the infidel textual theories of the leaders of religious apostasy in the eighteenth and nineteenth centuries. Like produces like and one has only to glance at the unfolding of the unbelieving "Higher Textual Criticism" to be struck by the unbelief of the textual theorists, the textual editors and the textual transmitters. Overwhelmingly they are found in the camp of the enemy who rejects that God ever gave to the world an Infallible Bible.

No Bible believer should be deceived by the parading of great names in the field of Biblical "scholarship", when these very men are but the parrots of the rationalists of another century. The case they present is not their own but a modern presentation of an ancient heresy. By lowering the Bible from the heaven of its divinity to depraved earth they declare it to be but an ordinary book of mere human production.

Robert L Dabney, the great Presbyterian scholar, was right when he castigated the modern texts upon which the English perversions of his day were based as coming from "the mind of infidel rationalism".

The theory of the producers and users of modern English perversions of Holy Scripture is that the Church of the Reformation, the Church of 1611 when the Authorized Version was published, and the church of the Great Evangelical Awakening, had not a true Bible. The foundation of their Bible, according to these critics, was not infallible. These great movements of God rest, according to modern translators, on a faulty and erroneous Bible.

It was only when Tischendorf discovered a manuscript in a trash-can, (used to hold papers to kindle the fire), in a cell of the Convent of St Catherine in Mt Sinai that at long last we had, according to them, a true text of the New Testament.

This manuscript of the New Testament was bound with portions of the Old Testament, the spurious Epistle of Barnabas and the spurious Epistle of the Shepherd of Hermas.

Think of it, the Almighty God who had promised to preserve His own Holy Word, allowed the majority of the copies to be destroyed until there were only two or three left. One of these was known to the monks as valueless, hence it was not in the library but in a trash-can - a reject indeed, being bound up with other spurious scriptures.

"The words of the Lord are pure words tried in a furnace of earth, purified seven times. Thou shalt keep them, O Lord, Thou shalt preserve them from this generation for ever." (Psalm 12:6-7)

While this imperfect and rejected copy was gathering dust, the Church of Christ was preaching out of copies of the true preserved Word of God. Souls were being gloriously saved and churches gloriously established, with the outpouring of the Holy Spirit upon them, the same Holy Spirit who divinely authored the Book.

The famous Dr F.H.A. Scrivener, the author of *A Full Collation of the Codex Sinaiticus* states: *"The text is covered with alterations of an obviously correctional character - brought in by at least ten different revisers, some of them systematically spread over every page by at least ten different revisers."*

So much for this so-called authoritative manuscript. Its imperfections and falsehoods are poxed on its very face.

The fact of such correction proves beyond doubt that the copy was always known to be erroneous.

These modern perversions all claim to rest partly upon this blighted and flawed manuscript. Evidently another such copy left is, according to the modern text theorists and defenders, the Codex Vaticanus.

This manuscript was discovered gathering dust in the Pope's library. Erasmus knew about this manuscript but although he was much nearer to the time of its production, he rejected it.

Rome set great obstacles against allowing the manuscript to be seen or copied. Rome always hated the Scriptures and while she was carefully concealing a mutilated text the true Church was preaching and proclaiming the preserved Word of God, and the kingdom of God was advancing among men.

Those who claimed they had found the true Word of God in the Antichrist's bookshelves in the 19th century, and set out to doctor all the Bibles in the world to conform them to the Roman imposture, only demonstrate their total ignorance of God's precious Word. From the Devil's bookstore they took the Devil's product and as sons of the father of lies they marketed its lie as truth. In fact they were peddling the Devil's lie. *God sent them a strong delusion that they should believe a lie that they all might be damned who believed not the truth but had pleasure in unrighteousness* (II Thessalonians 1:11-12).

The manuscript deletes among other Scriptures the last verses of Mark 16:9-20. All the attacks on that portion of Scripture are based on that deletion.

The basis of such rejection is without foundation, even with the Codex Vaticanus before us.

One of the foremost Biblical scholars of his day, John William Burgon (1813-1888) Dean of Chichester and champion in maintaining inviolate the inspiration and preservation of the Holy Scripture, brought to the attention of the whole world this fact about the Codex Vaticanus:

*"To say that in the Vatican Codex (B), which is unquestionably the oldest we possess, St Mark's Gospel ends abruptly at the eighth verse of the sixteenth chapter, and that the customary subscription (Kata Mapkon) follows, is true; but it is far from being the whole truth. It requires to be stated in addition that the scribe, whose plan is found to have been to begin every fresh book of the Bible at the top of the next ensuing column to that which contained the concluding words of the preceding book, has at the close of St Mark's Gospel deviated from his else invariable practice. He **has left in this place one column entirely vacant. It is the only vacant column in the whole manuscript - a blank space abundantly sufficient to contain the twelve verses which he nevertheless withheld.** Why did he leave that column vacant? What can have induced the scribe on this solitary occasion to depart from his established rule? The phenomenon (I believe I was the first to call distinct attention to it) is in the highest degree significant, and admits only one interpretation. **The older manuscript from which Codex B was copied must have infallibly contained the twelve verses in dispute.** The copyist was instructed to leave them out - and he obeyed; but he prudently left a blank space in memoriam rei. Never was blank more intelligible! **Never was silence more eloquent! By this simple expedient, strange to relate, the Vatican Codex is made to refute itself even while it seems to be bearing testimony against the concluding verses of St Mark's Gospel,** by withholding them; for it forbids the inference which, under ordinary*

circumstances, must have been drawn from that omission. It does more. **By leaving room for the verses it omits, it brings into prominent notice at the end of fifteen centuries and a half, a more ancient witness than itself.**
Revision Revised Edition: The last twelve verses of the Gospel of St. Mark- (pp. 86, 87)

John Burgon's testimony was absolutely unambiguous and crystal clear.

"Either, with the best and wisest of all ages, you must believe the whole of Holy Scripture or with the narrow-minded infidel, you must disbelieve the whole. There is no middle course"

Yes, let me emphasise that - there is no middle ground.

We either have a reliable Bible in our mother tongue or we have not.

What is the use of God verbally inspiring the Bible if He did not preserve it verbally for all generations?

Between a verbally inspired Bible and a verbally preserved Bible there is no middle ground. You cannot have the one without the other.

The Authorized Version rests on the foundation of the Received Traditional Text, the text of the centuries. The false foundation of the modern perversions is but the text of yesterday. The oldest is the best.

It is the Ancient Text. It is the text found in the great majority of the manuscript copies and the text read in the Greek church for over 1000 years.

Even Bishop Hort had to concede that the Received Text was "Quite as old as 350AD or older".

Bishop Charles Ellicott, the Head of the New Testament Revision Commission, stated:

"'The manuscripts which Erasmus used differ, for the most part, only in small and insignificant details from the bulk of the cursive manuscripts. The general character of their text is the same. **By this observation the pedigree of the Received Text is carried up beyond the individual manuscripts used by Erasmus ... That pedigree stretches back to a remote antiquity. The first ancestor of the Received Text was at least contemporary with the oldest of our extant manuscripts, if not older than any one of them.**'
- Charles John Ellicott, (The Revisers and the Greek Text of the New Testament, by Two Members of the New Testament Company, 1882, pp. 11, 12.)

Contrast this with the testimony of Robert Lewis Dabney, the outstanding Presbyterian leader of the Southern Presbyterians in the United States 1820-1898:

"The Vatican, the Alexandrine, and now the Sinai. **It is expressly admitted that neither of these has an extant history.** *No documentary external evidence exists as to the names of the copyists who transcribed them, the date, or the place of their writing.* **Nobody knows whence the Vatican MS came to the pope's library, or how long it has been there ... Tischendorf himself was unable to trace the presence of his favourite codex, in the monastery of St Catherine on Mt Horeb, by external witnesses higher than the twelfth century.** *THEIR EARLY DATE IS CONFESSEDLY ASSIGNED THEM BY CONJECTURE (conjectura: a casting together) of internal marks. It may be rightly assigned, yet by conjecture...*

The following list [of doctrinal corruptions in the critical Greek text] is not presented as complete, but as containing the most notable of these points ... the Sinai and the Vatican MSS, concur in omitting, in Matthew vi. 13, the closing doxology of our Lord's prayer. In John viii, 1-11, they and the Alexandrine omit the whole narrative of Christ's interview with the woman taken in adultery and her accusers. The first two omit the whole of Mark xvi., from the ninth verse to the end. Acts viii. 37, in which Philip is represented as propounding to the eunuch faith as the qualification for baptism, is omitted by all three ... in Acts ix. 5, 6 ... the Sinai, Vatican and Alexandrine MSS all concur in omitting "Who are thou, Lord? and the Lord said ..." from the passage.

In I Tim. iii. 16 ... the Sinai, Codex Ephremi, and probably the Alexandrine, ...

In I John v. 7 ... all the old MSS concur in omitting the heavenly witnesses ...

In Jude 4 ... the MSS omit God.

In Rev. i. 11 ... all three MSS under remark concur in omitting the Messiah's eternal titles ...

If now the reader will glance back upon this latter list of variations, he will find that in every case, the doctrinal effect of the departure from the received text is to obscure or suppress some testimony for the divinity of the Saviour.

The significant fact to which we wish especially to call attention is this: that all the variations proposed on the faith of these manuscripts which have any doctrinal importance, should attack the one doctrine of the Trinity; nay, we may say even more specifically, the one doctrine of Christ's deity ... Their admirers [of the favoured manuscripts supporting the critical text] claim for them an origin in the fourth or fifth century. The Sabellian and Arian controversies raged in the third and fourth. Is there no coincidence here? Things do not happen again and again regularly without a cause ... And when we remember the date of the great Trinitarian contest, and compare it with the supposed date of these exemplars of the sacred text, the ground of suspicion becomes violent ... **THESE VARIATIONS ARE TOO NUMERABLE, AND TOO SIGNIFICANT**

IN THEIR EFFECT UPON THE ONE DOCTRINE, TO BE ASCRIBED TO CHANCE.

... SOMEBODY HAS PLAYED THE KNAVE WITH THE TEXT ... We think that [the reader] will conclude with us that the weight of probability is greatly in favour of this theory that the anti-Trinitarians, finding certain codices in which these doctrinal readings had been already lost through the licentious criticism of Origen and his school, industrously diffuse them. While they also did what they dared to add to the omissions of similar readings.

- R L Dabney, "The Doctrinal Various Readings of the New Testament Greek," Southern Presbyterian Review, April 1871, reprinted in Discussions Evangelical and Theological, 1890, pp. 350-389

David Cloud in his well researched book *The Battle for the King James Version and the Received Text from 1800 to the Present* states six facts. These facts, which are stubborn things, have never budged in the hottest fire of this controversy.

1. The modern text flows from a stream of apostasy.

2. The manuscripts preferred by modern translators represent a rejected text.

3. The doctrines of inspiration and preservation secure a dependable Bible.

4. The Traditional Received Text is more theologically conservative than the modern critical text.

5. The rejection of the Traditional Received Text and the Authorized King James Version founded on it, has resulted in a multiplicity of modern texts and versions which have eroded the authority of God's Word.

6. To reject the Received Text and the King James is to reject the old paths.

Of Bishops Westcott and Hort, who sold the view of the unreliability of the Traditional Received Text and thus the Authorized Version, Zane Hodges notes, are easily found guilty of the charge of rationalism by the opening statements found in their introduction to *The New Testament In Original Greek*:

> "To begin with, Westcott and Hort are clearly unwilling to commit themselves to the inerrancy of the original Scriptures" - Hodges.

It was the conspiracy of Westcott and Hort to force secretly upon the Revised Version translators their new Greek Text which put the Revised Version off the rails and commenced the rash of English perversions of the Holy Scripture.

So dishonest was their behaviour that Charles Wordsworth, Bishop of St. Andrews, refused to sign his name to a testimonial of thanks to the Chairman because he was so discouraged by *"the number of minute and unnecessary changes made in direct violation of the instruction under which the work was undertaken."*

Looking back on the translation, the Bishop called it *"a deplorable failure"*.

It was however, more. It was a damnable conspiracy to set up false Bibles seeking to usurp the place of the one and only true Bible.

> *There exists no reason for supposing that the Divine Agent, who in the first instance thus gave to mankind the Scriptures of Truth, straightway abdicated His office; took no further care of His work; abandoned those precious writings to their fate. That a perpetual miracle was wrought for their preservation - that copyists were protected against the risk of error, or evil men prevented from altering shamefully, copies of the Deposit - no one, it is presumed, is so weak as to suppose. But it is quite a different thing to claim that* **ALL DOWN THE AGES THE SACRED WRITINGS MUST NEEDS HAVE BEEN GOD'S PECULIAR CARE; THAT THE CHURCH UNDER HIM HAS WATCHED OVER THEM WITH INTELLIGENCE**

AND SKILL; has recognised which copies exhibit a fabricated, which an honestly transcribed text; has generally sanctioned the one, and generally disallowed the other. **I am utterly disinclined to believe - so grossly improbable does it seem - that at the end of 1800 years 995 copies out of every thousand, suppose, will prove untrustworthy; and that the one, two, three, four or five which remain, whose contents were till yesterday as good as unknown, will be found to have retained the secret of what the Holy Spirit originally inspired. I am utterly unable to believe, in short, that God's promise has so entirely failed, that at the end of 1800 years much of the text of the Gospel has in point of fact to be picked by a German critic out of a waste-paper basket in the convent of St Catherine; and that the entire text had to be remodelled after the pattern set by a couple of copies which had remained in neglect during fifteen centuries, and had probably owed their survival to that neglect; whilst hundreds of others had been thumbed to pieces, and had bequeathed their witness to copies made from them.**

- John Burgon, The Traditional Text, pp. 11, 12

"*Strange as it may appear, it is undeniably true, that the whole of the controversy may be reduced to the following narrow issue: Does the truth of the Text of Scripture dwell with the vast multitude of copies, uncial and cursive, concerning which nothing is more remarkable than the marvellous agreement which subsists between them? Or is it rather to be supposed that the truth abides exclusively with a very little handful of manuscripts, which at once differ from the great bulk of the witnesses, and - strange to say - also amongst themselves?*" (ibid., p. 16)

The unfolding of time has demonstrated this more and more.

CALL THIS TEXT ERASMIAN OR COMPLUTENSIAN - THE TEXT OF STEPHENS, OR OF BEZA, OR OF THE ELZEVIRS - CALL IT THE "RECEIVED", OR THE "TRADITIONAL GREEK TEXT", OR WHATEVER

OTHER NAME YOU PLEASE - THE FACT REMAINS, THAT A TEXT HAS COME DOWN TO US WHICH IS ATTESTED BY A GENERAL CONSENSUS OF ANCIENT COPIES, ANCIENT VERSIONS, ANCIENT FATHERS.

- John Burgon, Revision Revised

OUR AUTHORIZED VERSION IS FOUNDED ON THAT ROCK.

THE FACT IS THAT THE FOUNDATION OF THE ENGLISH AUTHORIZED VERSION (KJV) OF THE HOLY BIBLE IS UNSURPASSABLY PRE-EMINENT IN THE UNDERLYING TEXTS UPON WHICH IT RESTS.

2. The foundation of the English Authorised Version (KJV) of the Holy Bible is unsurpassably pre-eminent in

the various English versions which gave it birth and of which it is the sum and substance, the pith and marrow, the essence, cream and perfection

The Authorized Version is not a new translation but rather a revision of a great number of English Bibles which went before. It owed its birth to a glorious train of English translations which came forth to bring to the English speaking people God's Holy Word.

Two great heroes of the faith - John Wycliffe and William Tyndale - more than a century separated - were the real pioneers of bringing the Bible to the English people in their own tongue.

Wycliffe set out to give to the common people the whole Bible in their own language and to encourage them to read it. If they could not read he set about teaching them to read.

Tennyson put the following words into the mouth of Sir John Oldcastle:

*"Not least art thou, thou little Bethlehem,
In Judah for in thee the Lord was born;
Nor thou in Britain little Lutterworth* (Wycliffe's work place)
Least, for in thee the Word was born again."

Wycliffe made the Bible the peoples' book and six centuries ago in 1382 caused the first complete English version of the Bible to be sent forth.

Once the Bible got into the hands of the English nation they have not let it be taken entirely away and, please God, never will.

This was before the invention of printing and every copy had to be handwritten. Nevertheless, a score of the original copies are still extant and copies of the originals number over one hundred.

The copies belonging to King Edward VI and Queen Elizabeth I are still in existence and both show evidence of constant use.

So much did the Bible influence the nation, it was stated that every other man in England became a Lollard (a believer in the Bible doctrines). Wycliffe's appeal was over the heads of the church hierarchy and scholars to the people themselves. The faith was delivered to the saints.

In 1408 the Church of Rome decreed that no man must ever again be permitted to translate the Bible into English nor read anything by Wycliffe without the permission of the Church. But Rome was too late. Freedom can never be overtaken once it has broken free. In the House of Commons to this day a painting by George Clausen RA depicting the people reading the Wycliffe Bible is on display, marking one of the epochs of English history.

Two great events then occurred which increased the demand for the Bible and enabled that demand to be met. One, the revival of learning; and two, the invention of printing.

Over one hundred years after the death of Wycliffe in 1384 William Tyndale was born. Eight years after his birth Columbas discovered America. When Luther nailed his theses at Wittenburg, Tyndale had already graduated from Oxford University.

Like Wycliffe, Tyndale saw the necessity of going over the heads of both Church and civil authorities to the people with the Bible in their own tongue. He stated that he would see to it that the ploughboys of England would know more of the Word of God than the priests of the realm.

Leaving England, Tyndale fled from place to place on the continent of Europe, with his life always in danger and many of his Bibles confiscated or burned.

In his book on the Authorized Version entitled *The Greatest English Classic,* Dr Cleland Boyd McAfee relates:

"There is one amusing story which tells how money came to free Tyndale from heavy debt and prepare the way for more Bibles. The Bishop of London, Tunstall, was set on destroying copies of the English New Testament. He therefore made a bargain with a merchant of Antwerp, Packington, to secure them for him. Packington was a friend of Tyndale, and went to him forthwith saying 'William, I know thou art a poor man, and I have gotten thee a merchant for thy books.' 'Who?' asked Tyndale. 'The Bishop of London.' 'Ah, but he will burn them.' 'So he will, but you will have the money.' And it all came out as it was planned; the Bishop of London had the books, Packington had the thanks, Tyndale had the money, the debt was paid, and the new edition was soon ready. The old document, from which I am quoting, adds that the Bishop thought he had God by the toe when, indeed, he found afterwards that he had the devil by the fist."

- pp 22-23

Tyndale's final revisions were published in 1534 and that was the notable year of his life. Two years afterwards he was strangled and burned. His martyrdom was achieved by the power of the Church and the State.

Tyndale's version was bound to be an epoch-making version. It was the first English version translated from the original Hebrew and Greek texts. This contrasted with Wycliffe, for his was a translation of the Latin Vulgate, itself a translation. Tyndale was a scholarly linguist, skilled in Hebrew, Greek, Latin, Italian, Spanish and French as well as his own mother tongue.

One year after Tyndale had cried out in martyrdom, "Lord, open the King of England's eyes!" the Lord opened the King of England's eyes and two versions of the Bible in English were licensed by the King of England and made available to the people.

The first Bible had been issued secretly two years before by Miles Coverdale, and was called (for no real reason) the Matthew Bible. The second was known as the Great Bible, a revision of the Matthew Bible, and was printed in France. Its entire edition was only saved by being shipped to England under the guise of waste paper having been confiscated by Rome's Inquisitor General.

Henry VIII died but the English Bible lived on. Under Edward VI and Thomas Cranmer the Archbishop of Canterbury, the Bible was reinstated in the parish churches and in the six years of the young king's short reign many editions were published.

Then Bloody Mary came to the throne and stopped the Bible's progress. But her ascent to the throne led to the production of one of the best of the early English Bibles, the famous Genevan Version produced by English exiles and patronised by the two Johns - Calvin and Knox.

The Genevan Bible became the most popular, and Queen Elizabeth, who had no time for Knox and Calvin, instructed her Archbishop of Canterbury to produce an authorised version. That edition became known as the Bishop's Bible. The Bishop's Bible was the immediate predecessor of the Authorized Version and the Authorized Version revised the same.

J W Wittaker MA, Fellow of St John's, Cambridge in 1820 in his authoritative work, *"An Historical and Critical Enquiry into the Interpretation of the Hebrew Scripture,"* gives the credentials of the translators of this Bible.

"Fortunately we are not left in ignorance of the attainments of these learned men, and the names of some of them would be sufficient evidence of the care with which this translation was conducted. Dr William Alley, Bishop of Exeter, was educated at King's College, from which place he went to Oxford, and there wrote a Hebrew Grammar. Dr Richard Davies, Bishop of St David's, to which See he was promoted from St Asaph, had been employed in translating the Bible into Welsh in conjunction with one Morgan, which employment he probably forsook when the English version required his assistance. Dr Edward Sandys was Bishop of Worcester, afterwards of London, and ultimately Archbishop of York. He, as well as Dr Robert Horne, Bishop of Winchester, received his education at St John's College, Cambridge; and Strype says that 'he was a man well skilled in the original languages'. In a letter which he wrote to the Archbishop, he complains that the Hebrew had not everywhere been diligently followed in the Great Bible, and that too great attention had been paid to Munster's Latin translation. Dr Thomas Bentham, Bishop of Lichfield and Coventry, had been Fellow of Magdalene College in Oxford, and during his residence there, Antony Woods says that "he did solely addict his mind to the study of theology, and to the learning of the Hebrew language." Being ejected from his fellowship in Queen Mary's reign [because of persecution], he retired to foreign countries and became a preacher at Zurich and Basle, but returned on the accession of Queen Elizabeth. The Book of Psalms passed through the hands of Dr Cox, Bishop of Ely, and perhaps some other persons. Possibly this Prelate may have been originally appointed by Parker, since Bentham was not nominated by the Archbishop, but by the Queen. Dr Edmund Grindall was educated at Magdalene College in Cambridge, and, as well as Bentham, resided abroad during Queen Mary's reign. On his return he was made Bishop of London, and afterwards Archbishop of Canterbury. His literary attainments in every branch of theological learning have never been doubted, and have been so well described by his biographer, Strype, that to enlarge here upon them would be superfluous"

- Wittaker, pp. 66-67

On Elizabeth's death James VI of Scotland became James I of England. At a conference of clergy which he convened at Hampton Court, and which evidently ended in complete division, there came one unanimous decision - to prepare a new edition of the English Bible. This edition was to harvest the crop of all the other English versions and to follow the Bishop's Bible wherever they could do so favourably, preference to be given to a familiar phrase rather than change, unless accuracy demanded it.

When the new version was published it was abundantly demonstrated that William Tyndale was the real father of the work.

About eighty percent of his Old Testament and ninety percent of his New Testament have been transferred to our version. In the Beatitudes, for example, five are word for word in the two versions, while the other three are only slightly changed. Dr Davidson has calculated that nine-tenths of the words in the shorter New Testament epistles are Tyndale's, and in the longer epistles like the Hebrews five-sixths are his. Froude's estimate is fair: *"Of the translation itself, though since that time it has been many times revised and altered, we may say that it is substantially the Bible with which we are familiar. The peculiar genius which breathes through it, the mingled tenderness and majesty, the Saxon simplicity, the preternatural grandeur, unequalled, unapproached, in the attempted improvements of modern scholars, all are here, and bear the impress of the mind of one man, William Tyndale."*

The Authorized Version then is *"the work not of one man, not of one age, but of many labourers, of diverse and even opposing views, over a period of ninety years. It was watered by the blood of the martyrs and its slow growth gave time for the casting off of imperfections and for the full accomplishment of its destiny as the Bible of the English nation."* - Frederic Kenyan in *Our Bible and the Ancient Manuscripts*.

THE FACT IS THAT THE ANCESTRY OF THE ENGLISH AUTHORIZED VERSION (KJV) OF THE HOLY BIBLE IS UNSURPASSABLY PRE-EMINENT IN THE VARIOUS ENGLISH VERSIONS WHICH GAVE IT BIRTH AND OF WHICH IT IS THE SUM AND SUBSTANCE, THE PITH AND MARROW, THE ESSENCE, CREAM AND PERFECTION.

3. The translators of the English Authorised Version (KJV) of the Holy Bible are pre-eminent in

their saintliness and scholarship, the providential way they were so singularly brought together, and the dedication with which they undertook and gloriously completed their mammoth task.

It was on the second day of the Hampton Court conference, January 16th, 1604, that Dr Reynolds, president of Corpus Christi College, Oxford, a moderate Puritan, raised the matter.

This Dr Reynolds, by the way, was party to a most curious episode. He had been an ardent Roman Catholic, and he had a brother who was an equally ardent Protestant. They argued with each other so earnestly that each convinced the other; the Roman Catholic became a Protestant, and the Protestant became a Roman Catholic!

As James hated what he termed the "republican Genevan Version" it became his fancy to manage the production of what he hoped would be the version of all English versions.

He little thought how well those whom he had appointed would succeed in the task given them by the one who was known as *"the greatest fool in Christendom"*.

John Richard Green, the historian, describes James thus:

His big head, his slobbering tongue, his quilted clothes, his rickety legs stood out in as grotesque a contrast with all that men recalled of Henry and Elizabeth as his gabble and rhodomontade, his want of personal dignity, his buffoonery, his coarseness of speech, his pedantry, his contemptible cowardice. Under this ridiculous exterior, however, lay a man of much natural ability, a ripe scholar with a considerable fund of shrewdness, of mother wit and ready repartee.

Before the year 1604 had run its course James had appointed fifty-four of the greatest Bible scholars of the realm to make the new version.

The plan of the work was that those appointed were to sit in six companies, two at Oxford, two at Cambridge and two at Westminster.

THE FIRST COMPANY

The list of the learned persons to whom the execution of the new version was entrusted has been carefully preserved and often published. It includes the names of some of the most distinguished of that day, whose memory is still dear to the friends of piety and literature; and as to others among them, of whom history has preserved scarcely any memorial, no reasonable doubt can be entertained of their competency to discharge their momentous trust. They were divided into six parties, two of which met in Oxford, two in Cambridge, and two in Westminster.

The first company, ten in number, met at Westminster, and to them were assigned the Pentateuch and the other historical books, as far as the end of the Second Book of Kings.

The principal individual, and the president of this company, was the celebrated Dr Launcelot Andrews, at the time of his appointment to the office of translator, Dean of Westminster, and afterwards promoted successively to the Sees of Chichester, Ely, and Winchester. Scholars of the greatest eminence, such as Casaubon, Grotius, and Vossius, have eulogised his extensive attainments; and the prelate Buckeridge, Bishop of Rochester, who preached the sermon at his funeral stated that he understood fifteen languages. He died in 1626, and Milton, in one of his early and beautiful Latin elegies, has embalmed the name of this distinguished scholar, and bewailed his loss in terms expressive of his wide and brilliant frame. The next translator on the list is Dr John Overall. He was a fellow of Trinity College, Cambridge; and in 1596 was raised to the Regius Professorship of Divinity in that university. In 1604 he was appointed to the deanery of St Paul's, and afterwards was preferred to the bishopric of Lichfield and Coventry, whence he was translated to the See of Norwich. It is said that to his eminent learning he was indebted for his great preferments. He died in 1619. Dr Andrain de Saravia, a learned foreigner of Spanish extraction, was the third person in the Westminster company. He had been Professor of Divinity in the University of Leyden, and after he became resident in England his attainments attracted the notice of Archbishop Whitgift, who appointed him successively to prebendal stall at Gloucester, Canterbury and Westminster. He died in 1613. Wood speaks of him as "educated in all kinds of literature in his younger days, especially in several languages." The fourth name given in the list of those at Westminster is that of Dr Richard Clarke, who had been fellow of Christ Church, Cambridge, and was, at the time of his appointment to the translatorship, vicar of Mynstre and Monkton, in the Isle of Thanet, and one of the six preachers at Canterbury Cathedral. A volume of learned sermons by this divine was published after his death, in 1637. Dr John Layfield, fellow of Trinity College, Cambridge, and rector of St Clement Danes, is the fifth on the list. Collier says, that being skilled in architecture, his judgment was much relied on for the fabric of the tabernacle and the temple. The sixth is Dr Teigh. He was Archdeacon of Middlesex, and Vicar of All Hallows, Barking, - "an excellent textuary and a profound linguist," according to the testimony of Wood, and therefore employed in the translation of the Bible. Mr Burgley, of Stretford, Mr Geoffrey King, Fellow of King's College, Cambridge, and Regius Professor of Hebrew; Mr Richard Thompson, of Clare Hall; and William Bedwell, of St John's College, in the same University, were other members of the first Westminster company. Of none of these individuals, except the last, has history preserved any further information. The name of Bedwell, however, is mentioned with great honour in the life of Dr Peacock. That famous oriental scholar is there stated to have been a pupil of Bedwell, "to whom the praise of being the first who considerably *promoted the study of the Arabic language in Europe may perhaps more justly belong, than to Thomas Erpinius who commonly has it."* He spent many years in preparing an Arabic lexicon; and the commencement of a Persian dictionary and an Arabic Translation of the Catholic Epistles of St John, by the same scholar, are still preserved among the Laud MSS in the Bodleian Library.

THE SECOND COMPANY

The second company, to whom was committed the books of the Old Testament from the beginning of Chronicles to the end of Canticles, met at Cambridge to pursue their labours. The president of this party was Edward Lively, Regius Professor of Hebrew at Cambridge, who enjoyed the reputation of an acquaintance with the oriental languages unequalled at that period. He died in 1605, and his death is supposed by some to have been hastened by the earnest attention which he devoted to his high commission immediately on his appointment. John Richardson, a fellow of Emanuel College, Cambridge, and afterwards Master of Peterhouse, and then of Trinity, was associated with Lively in the company of the Cambridge translators. Next to him was Dr Laurence Chaderton, one of the Cambridge delegates to the Hampton Court conference. He was Fellow of Christ's College, and afterwards Master of Emanuel. Chaderton entered Christ's College in 1564 and embraced the Reformed doctrines. He had been brought up as a Roman Catholic, and his father offered him an allowance of thirty pounds if he would leave Cambridge and renounce Protestantism - "Otherwise I enclose a shilling to buy a wallet - to go and beg." He acquired a great reputation as a Latin, Greek and Hebrew scholar and was also proficient in French, Spanish and Italian. It is remarkable that after having, when advanced in life, from fear of the appointment of a successor of Arminian principles, resigned his mastership in favour of one who held the same opinions with himself, he not only survived this person, but lived to see two other masters. He died in 1640, at the age of ninety-four. He is described as well-skilled in Latin, Greek and Hebrew; but to the study of Rabbinical learning he especially devoted himself, with a view to the elucidation of the Scripture. He was one of the three representative Puritans at the Hampton Court conference. Forty clergy owed their confession to his preaching. Of Francis Dillingham, fourth on the Cambridge list, all we know is that he was Fellow of Christ's College, Parson of Dean in Bedfordshire, and author of some theological pieces. According to

Fuller, "He was an excellent linguist". He wrote A Dissuasive Against Popery."

Little is known of Thomas Harrison, the next name that appears. He was vice-master of Trinity College, and his attainments in Hebrew are indicated by his having been appointed by the University as chief examiner in that language. The names of Roger Andrews, brother of the Bishop, Fellow of Pembroke Hall, Master of Jesus College, and Prebendary of Chichester and Southwell. He is described in the Lambeth manuscript as having been also Vicar of Chigwell, Essex and Cuckfield, Sussex. He was made BD 1604; DD 1609. Robert Spalding, a Fellow of St John's College, and successor to Lively in the Hebrew chair - and Dr Andrew Byng, Fellow of Peterhouse, and afterwards successor to Mr King, who followed Spalding in the same professorship, close the list of the second company of translators.

THIRD COMPANY

The third company met at Oxford, and consisted of only seven persons, to whom was allotted the rest of the Old Testament from Isaiah to Malachi.

Dr John Harding, described as father-in-law to Dr Reynolds (Lambeth MS), president of Magdalene College, Regius Professor of Hebrew, and Rector of Halsey, in Oxfordshire, presided over this company. Dr John Reynolds, already mentioned as a chief advocate on the Puritan side at the Hampton Court conference, and the person who suggested the new version to King James, was conspicuous among the Oxford translators. In 1598 he became President of Corpus Christi, which station he held at the time of his death, in 1607. His learning is particularly noticed by Wood; and Hall relates that the memory in reading of the man were near to a miracle. Dr Thomas Holland was the next member of the party at Oxford. He was Fellow of Balliol College, Rector of Exeter, and Regius Professor of Divinity; and was particularly qualified for the work of translation, inasmuch as he had the character of being another Apollos - mighty in the Scriptures. He died in 1612. He was no man for episcopacy. (Lambeth MS.) Dr Richard Kilby's name stands fourth in the list. He was rector of Lincoln College, and author of Commentaries on Exodus, prepared chiefly from the writings of the Rabbis and Hebrew interpreters. Good old Isaac Walton relates the following anecdote of Kilby, in connection with his employment on the Authorized Version: - "The Doctor was to ride a journey into Derbyshire, and took Mr Sanderson to bear him company; and they, going together on a Sunday with the doctor's friend to that parish church where they then were, found the young preacher to have no more discretion than to waste a great part of the hour alotted for his sermon in exceptions against the late translation of several words, not expecting such a hearer as Dr Kilby, and showed three reasons why a particular word should have been otherwise translated. When evening prayer was ended, the preacher was invited to the doctor's friend's house, where, after some other conference, the doctor told him he might have preached more useful doctrine, and not have filled his auditors' ears with needless exceptions against the late translation; and for that word for which he offered to that poor congregation three reasons why it ought to have been translated as he said, he and others had considered all of them, and found thirteen more considerable reasons why it was translated as now printed." This circumstance was enough to cure the young divine of his fondness for criticism in the pulpit. Dr Miles Smith, who took a leading part in the translation, and who afterwards wrote the Preface, was of the Oxford company. He was at the time Canon of Hereford, and for his indefatigable exertions in forwarding the version, was elevated to the See of Gloucester. Wood speaks of him as having Hebrew at his finger's ends, and as being so conversant in Chaldee, Syriac, and Arabic, that he made them as familiar to him almost as his native tongue. Making some allowance in this case as in others for the somewhat extravagant character of the Oxford historian's eulogies, they are still to be considered as trustworthy testimonies to the very superior scholarship of these ornaments of his Alma Mater. He authored the long translators' preface to the version. De Brett, of Lincoln College, Oxford, and Rector of Quainton, in Buckinghamshire, - a good Grecian, an oriental scholar, and famous alike for learning and piety, - and Mr Fairclough, complete the number of this company of the translators at Oxford.

THE FOURTH COMPANY

The fourth company, consisting of eight members, also met at Oxford, and to them were committed the four Gospels, the Acts of the Apostles, and the Revelation of John.

Dr Thomas Ravis, (He took all academical degrees, and enjoyed all collegiate dignities. He was student, Canon, and Dean of Christ Church, Chaplain to Archbishop Whitgift, vice-chancellor of Oxford, Bishop of Gloucester, 1604, and of London 1607. He died December 14th, 1609. He was a great man against the ministers who petitioned King James. (Lambeth MS.) then Dean of Christ Church, and afterwards successively Bishop of Gloucester and London, was the president. His eminent learning is mentioned by Wood. George Abbot, Dean of Winchester, but better known as Archbishop of Canterbury, to which elevated station he was raised in the same year that the version was published, was also one of the second class which met at Oxford. Though the singular events of his life, and the active part which he took in the ecclesiastical and political affairs of the day, impart to him his chief distinction on the page of history, there can be no doubt that he was a very superior scholar, or he would not have enjoyed, as he did, the honour of filling three times the office of vice-chancellor of his University. He very strongly opposed the Romanising influence of Laud and was very severe in his denunciation of anything which savoured of "popery".

Nevertheless he accepted some high offices in the Church of England and in 1609 became Bishop of Lichfield and Archbishop of Canterbury in 1611. He was regarded as the head of the Puritans within the Church of England and he vigorously opposed the King's declaration permitting sports and pastimes on the Lord's Day. He encouraged James to request the States General to dismiss Vorstius from his professorship at Leyden because of his Arminianism.

Dr Richard Eedes, Dean of Worcester, another of the translators of this class, died very soon after his appointment in 1604. "Mr Dean of Worcester" is the name in the original list; Dr Eedes was Dean of Worcester at the time of his death, in 1604, and he must be the person intended. Wood expressly states that Dr Eedes was one of the translators. Ath. Ox. Dr Giles Tomson, Dean of Windsor, and afterwards Bishop of Gloucester, the fourth of the Oxford company, was a man of high reputation for learning, as well as an eminent preacher. Mr Saville's name comes next. This was, no doubt, Sir Henry Saville, Tutor in Greek to Queen Elizabeth, appointed by her to be Provost of Eton College in 1596, and knighted by King James in 1604. Wood observes that the encomiums given of him by divers authors would, if enumerated, form a manual. John Perin, Greek Professor, and a noted Latinist, Grecian, and divine, a solid theologian, and an *elegant orator of the English language for the age in which he lived, were the remaining individuals employed at Oxford in the preparation of the version.*

FIFTH COMPANY

The next class, consisting of seven individuals, assembled at Westminster and translated the Epistles of Paul, and the general Epistles. William Barlowe, Dean of Chester, afterwards Bishop of Rochester, and finally of Lincoln, is the only one of whom much is known. He was one of the divines at the Hampton Court conference, of which he wrote an account, not so impartial as it ought to be, according to the admission of Fuller in his Church History. Of the five following names no biographical particulars have been discovered; Dr Hutchenson, Dr Spencer, Mr Fenton, Mr Rabbetts, and Mr Sanderson. The last on the list is Mr Dakins, Professor of Divinity in Gresham College.

SIXTH COMPANY

The sixth and last company met at Cambridge. They comprised the following persons: Dr John Duport, Prebendary of Ely, and afterwards master of Jesus College, Cambridge, also four times vice-chancellor of the University; Dr Branthwaite, at that time Fellow of Emanuel College, afterwards Master of Gonville and Caius College, Cambridge; Dr Jeremiah Radcliffe, Fellow of Trinity College, in the same University; Dr Samuel Ward, at that time of Emanuel College, and afterwards Master of Sidney College, and Lady Margaret Professor of Divinity. He was the correspondent of Archbishop Usher; and his letters are said to unfold treasures of diversified learning, especially concerning biblical and oriental criticism. Andrew Downes, Greek Professor at Cambridge, whose notes on Chrysostom are particularly commended in Usher's letters. John Bois or Boys, Fellow of St John's College, Prebendary of Ely, and Rector of Boxworth, near Cambridge. He was extremely well acquainted with the Hebrew language, and his knowledge of Greek was equally great. When the work was completed John Boys was one of the six translators who met at Stationers Hall to revise the whole. This took them about nine months and during this period the Company of Stationers made them an allowance of thirty shillings each per week. Some of the notes made by John Boys during the final revision were recently discovered in Corpus Christi College Library at Oxford, edited by Professor Ward Allen, and published in 1970 under the title - "Translating for King James". John Boys' "Exposition of the Epistles and Gospels used in the English Liturgy" furnishes ample evidence of his competent scholarship and doctrinal soundness. After a long life of profitable study, ministry, translating and writing, he died at the age of 84, "his brow without wrinkles, his sight quick, his hearing sharp, his countenance fresh and his body sound". Mr Ward, Fellow of King's College, Cambridge, Prebendary of Chichester, and Rector of Bishop's Waltham in Hampsire, completes the list.

With great faithfulness these dedicated men did their colossal task. None were paid. They laboured for the benefit of others and not themselves. Three years they spent on the original work, three years of careful revision and on the marginal references. Then in six months a committee reviewed it all, put it through the press and at last in 1611 it appeared Authorized and Appointed to be read in the churches and bearing the imprint of Robert Barker, printer to the King's Most Excellent Majesty.

It was never authorized officially by any statutory authority, neither did King or Archbishop appoint it to be read in the churches. Its reception and its eventual pre-eminence over all other versions by the approval of the people silenced all its carping critics.

No wonder Joseph Charles Philpot, 1802-1869, the illustrious leader of the Gospel Standard Baptists and a Fellow of Worcester College, Oxford, in answer to the question - Who are to undertake a revision of the Authorized (KJV) today? replied:

> "Of course they must be learned men, great critics, scholars, and divines. But these are notoriously either tainted with popery or infidelity. Where are the men, learned, yet sound in Truth, not to say alive unto God, who possess the necessary qualifications for so important work? And can erroneous men, dead in trespasses and sins, carnal, worldly, ungodly persons, spiritually translate a Book written by the blessed Spirit? We have not the slightest ground for hope that they would be godly men, such as we have reason to believe translated the Scriptures into our present version."

THE FACT IS, THE TRANSLATORS OF THE AUTHORIZED VERSION (KJV) OF THE ENGLISH BIBLE ARE UNSURPASSABLY PRE-EMINENT IN 1, THEIR SAINTLINESS AND SCHOLARSHIP; 2, IN THE PROVIDENTIAL WAY THEY WERE SO SINGULARLY BROUGHT TOGETHER; AND 3, THE DEDICATION WITH WHICH THEY UNDERTOOK AND COMPLETED THEIR MAMMOTH TASK.

4 The translation of the English Authorised Version (KJV) of the Holy Bible is unsurpassably pre-eminent in *the techniques it employed*

The Authorized Version was born in an age of faith. Its inception and reception is characterised by that faith. It is both the Believer's Book and the Believing Book.

The Bible is God's Book, not man's, and must be handled in its translation as God's Text and not as a common man-made text.

Dr Edward F Hills, prominent Presbyterian minister and author of the masterly *King James Version Defended* states:

"In the realm of New Testament textual criticism as well as in other fields the presuppositions of modern thought are hostile to the historic Christian faith and will destroy it if their fatal operation is not checked. If faithful Christians, therefore, would defend their sacred religion against this danger, **they must forsake the foundations of unbelieving thought and build upon their faith,** *a faith that rests entirely on the solid rock of Holy Scripture. And when they do this in the sphere of New Testament textual criticism,* **they will find themselves led back step by step (perhaps, at first, against their wills)** *to the text of the*

Protestant Reformation, namely, that form of New Testament text which underlies the King James Version and the other early Protestant translations."

- Edward F Hills, The King James Bible Defended, Introduction, 3rd ed., 1979, p.1

"... the Bible version which you use ... has already been decided for you by the workings of God's special providence. If you ignore this providence and choose to adopt one of these modern versions, you will be taking the first step in the logic of unbelief. For the arguments which you must use to justify your choice are the same arguments which unbelievers use to justify theirs, the same method. If you adopt one of these modern versions, you must adopt the naturalistic New Testament textual criticism upon which it rests. This naturalistic textual criticism requires us to study the New Testament text in the same way in which we study the texts of secular books which have not been preserved by God's special providence."

- Hills, Believing Bible Study, Des Moines, Iowa: Christian Research Press, 1967, pp. 226, 227

The Authorized Version's translators approached the Bible with reverence and godly fear knowing it to be God's Holy Word given to sinful man for his salvation. They did not treat it as man-orientated, they reverenced it as God-originated. That is why in their translation work they adopted special techniques from which they refused to depart.

THE FIRST TECHNIQUE WAS FIDELITY

There could be no fiddling with the Divine Book. God's Word was not for changing. There was no twisting of the text to please the patronage of King James. They might be subjects of the King but they were slaves of the Bible. The Bible was not a Puritan Book or a High Church Book. No matter who was offended or who was pleased the truth must be told. Their version said in English exactly what it said in Hebrew or Greek, nothing less, nothing more. It was not an interpretation nor an explanation.

The translators were not prepared to twist any text to make it serve the will of their royal patron King James.

To handle the Scriptures with fidelity and to maintain faithful translation all the way through, was a translation technique never before insisted upon and faithfully maintained.

Dr. McAfee comments:

"Now, if anyone thinks that is easy, or only a matter of course, he plainly shows that he has never been a theologian or a scholar in a contested field. Ask any lawyer whether it is easy to handle his authorities with entire impartiality, whether it is a matter of course that he will let them say just what they meant to say when his case is involved. Of course, he will seek to do it as an honest lawyer, but equally, of course, he will have to keep close watch on himself or he will fail in doing it. Ask any historian whether it is easy to handle the original documents in a field in which he has firm and announced opinions, and to let those documents speak exactly what they mean to say, whether they support him or not. The greater historians will always do it, but they will sometimes do it with a bit of a wrench.

Even a scholar is human, and these men sitting in their six companies would all have to meet this Book afterwards and have their opinions tried by it. There must have been times when some of them would be inclined to salt the mine a little, to see that it would yield what they would want it to yield later. So far as these men were able to do it, they made it say in English just what it said in Hebrew and Greek. They showed no inclination to use it as a weapon in their personal warfare."

- pp 65-66

THE SECOND TECHNIQUE WAS FEALTY

This is the oath-bound loyalty on the part of a vassal to his lord. Such was the translators' oath-bound commitment to the Word of God which He (God) had *magnified above all His name*. "I will worship toward thy holy temple, and praise thy name for thy lovingkindness and for thy truth: for thou hast magnified thy word above all thy name" (Psalm 138:2).

This fealty compelled them to make plain, beyond the shadow of a doubt, that where there were no words in the original to correspond with those English words used in the translation to bring out the accurate meaning, they had all those words printed carefully in italics to distinguish them.

Here was a total commitment to the verbal inspiration of the Bible, demonstrated on every page of the Authorized Version. What other translation has such fealty?

Dean Burgon is well worth quoting here with regard to verbal inspiration:

"I am asked whether I believe the words of the Bible to be inspired, I answer, To be sure I do, - every one of them: and every syllable likewise. Do not you? Where, (if it be a fair question,) where do you, in your wisdom, stop? The book, you allow, is inspired. How about the chapters? How about the verses? Do you stop at the verses, and not go on to the words? ... **No, Sirs! THE BIBLE (BE PERSUADED) IS THE VERY UTTERANCE OF THE ETERNAL; - AS MUCH GOD'S WORD, AS IF HIGH HEAVEN WERE OPEN, AND WE HEARD GOD SPEAKING TO US WITH HUMAN VOICE.** *Every book of it, is inspired alike; and* ***is inspired entirely*** *...* **THE BIBLE IS NONE OTHER THAN THE VOICE OF HIM THAT SITTETH UPON THE THRONE! EVERY BOOK OF IT, - EVERY CHAPTER OF IT, - EVERY VERSE OF IT, - EVERY WORD OF IT, - EVERY SYLLABLE OF IT, - (WHERE ARE WE TO STOP?) - EVERY LETTER OF IT - IS THE DIRECT UTTERANCE OF THE MOST HIGH!** *... Well spake the Holy Ghost, by the mouth of the many blessed men who wrote it. -* **The Bible is none other than the Word of God: not some part**

of it, more, some part of it less; but all alike, the utterance of Him who sitteth upon the Throne;- absolute, - faultless, - unerring, - supreme! "

- Sermon III, pp.75, 76, 89

Because every word of the Bible is absolute - faultless - unerring - supreme, the Authorized Version translators introduced the italic print technique.

John Charles Philpot, the Oxford-educated scholar and Fellow and a Master in the Hebrew and Greek text gives this testimony:

*"**We cannot but admire the great faithfulness of our translators in so scrupulously adhering to the exact words of the Holy Spirit**, and when they were necessarily compelled to supply the ellipses in the original, to point out that they had done so by making the word in italic characters. By so doing, they engaged themselves, as by bond, **TO GIVE THE WORD OF GOD IN ITS STRICT ORIGINAL PURITY**; and yet, as thorough scholars in the original tongues, and complete masters of their own, **THEY WERE ENABLED TO GIVE US A VERSION ADMIRABLE NOT ONLY FOR ITS STRICT FIDELITY, BUT FOR ITS ELOQUENCE, GRANDEUR, AND BEAUTY.**"*

THE THIRD TECHNIQUE WAS HUMILITY

The translators did not enter upon their task robed with majesty, but rather clad in humility.

They made use of all available knowledge in the field, and took advantage from friend and foe alike. Even their supreme critic, Hugh Broughton, maddened by not being appointed to serve with them, without his will was conscripted to help. His already contribution in translation of certain Scriptures was harnessed. Several of the capital phrases in the Version are from his pen.

"Truly Christian Reader," they informed their constituency, *"we never thought from the beginning that we would need to make a new translation, nor*

yet to make a bad one a good one, but to make a good one better. That has been our endeavour, that our work."

One line of this humility is worth careful consideration.

As we have already noticed, the translators were not explainers or expositors of the text but purely translators. Theirs was no argumentative purpose. Their work was not apologetic (that is defensive of doctrine) their work was to state as simply and plainly as they could the doctrine revealed in the Word of God. It was simply an out-and-out translation. They translated the text as it was set down, bowing in humility before its exalted sovereignty.

In setting it down they hunted every available quarter, ransacking *"all English forms for felicitous words and happy phrases."*

There was no desire to break new ground, preference was always given to a familiar phrase rather than a new one, unless accuracy demanded it.

The Hebrew and Greek texts, the English versions which went before them, back to Wycliffe, (although his was a translation from the Latin Vulgate) and the other translation into other tongues, including the Septuagint, the oldest translation of the Old Testament Hebrew into the Greek. These included Luther's German Bible, which did for the German tongue what their version was destined to do for the English tongue. Other men laboured and they, for the greater good, joyfully entered into their labours. Above it all however, was the overwhelming radiance of William Tyndale, the martyr.

Another line of this humility was calling into use *the technique of transliteration*.

Where certain points were matters of legitimate controversy and unsettled, the translators moved with care not to commit themselves to any interpretation. They used instead the technique of transliteration, that is, they brought the Hebrew or Greek word over letter by letter into the English. In so doing, they refused to make the Bible a denominational or party book. Rather, bowing to its infallibility, they wrote into it the very inspired Word of the original.

This was done with the proper names, especially of the Old Testament, because most Old Testament names can be translated. For example Adam is the Hebrew word for man; David, the Hebrew for beloved and Malachi for My Messenger.

The translators in this area rightly kept to the transliteration technique.

Again, Dr. McAfee points out:

"In this connection it is well to notice the effort of the King James trans-lators at the fair statement of the Divine Name. It will be remembered that it appears in the Old Testament ordinarily as "LORD", printed in small capitals. A very interesting bit of verbal history lies back of that word. The word which represents the Divine Name in Hebrew consists of four consonants, j, or y, h, v, and h. There are no vowels; indeed, there were no vowels in the early Hebrew at all. Those that we now have were added not far from the time of Christ. No one knows the original pronunciation of that sacred name consisting of four letters. At a very early day it had become too sacred to pronounce, so that when men came to reading it or in speech they simply used another word which is translated into English, Lord, a word of high dignity. When the time came that vowels were to be added to the consonants, the vowels of this other word Lord were placed under the consonants of the sacred name, so that in the word Jehovah, where the jhvh occur, there are the consonants of one word whose vowels are unknown and the vowels of another word whose consonants are not used.

These translators had to face that problem. It was a peculiar problem at that time. How should they put into English the august name of God when they did not know what the true vowels were? There was dispute among the scholars. They did not take sides as our later American Revision has done, some of us think quite unwisely. They chose to retain the Hebrew usage, and print the Divine Name in unmistakable type so that its personal meaning could not be mistaken."

- pp 69-71

THE FOURTH TECHNIQUE WAS CONTEXTUALITY

The translators used the principle advocated by Purvey who completed the Wycliffe version namely, *"The best translation is translated after the sentence and not word by word as the sentence goes along. This makes the sentence one in both languages."*

It is quite possible to put any language over, literally translating word by word but the end result would be great inaccuracy. The grammar and syntax are of vital importance for accuracy.

This contextuality covered not only the immediate words in a sentence but covered the whole Bible through the translators amassing the marginal readings. To them the context of any text is the whole of the rest of the Bible. They were absolutely assured of the Bible's absolute unity.

THE FIFTH TECHNIQUE WAS VARIETY

The translators sought to put the meaning into English terms and shunned a slavish uniformity.

For example in James 2:2-3 one Greek word is translated in three different ways - apparel - raiment - clothing. It was this technique of variety which made the Authorized Version an English Bible indeed, preserving for us the Word of God in our mother tongue.

For example, the word might be either "journeying or travelling" or "eternal or everlasting" but both express in English the proper sense of the original.

One of the reasons the translators gave for this variety is quite unique. Again, it recognised the great honour imparted to English words to convey the very Word of the only true and living God. It demonstrates once more the reverent way in which they went about their task.

McAfee states:

"They said they did not think it right to honour some words by giving them a place forever in the Bible, while they virtually said to other equally good words: "Get ye hence and be banished forever." They quote a "certaine great philosopher" who said that those logs were happy which became images and were worshipped, while other logs as good as they were laid behind the fire to be burned. So they sought to use as many English words, familiar in speech and commonly understood, as they might, lest they should impoverish the language, and so lose out of use good words."

- p 77

THE FACT IS, THE TRANSLATION OF THE ENGLISH AUTHORIZED VERSION (KJV) OF THE BIBLE IS UNSURPASSABLY PRE-EMINENT IN THE TECHNIQUES IT EMPLOYED.

5 The language of the English Authorised Version (KJV) of the Holy Bible is unsurpassably pre-eminent
being the first from the well undefiled and indeed the very well itself

Every living language is communicated in three levels of speech.

First, there is the level of intelligentsia - the cleverest scientists, the clearest thinkers and the most careful writers. We would call that the upper level. This level is remote in many ways from the habitual speech of common life.

Second, there is the level of the least educated of our people. Their speech is rough, often incorrect grammatically, well flavoured with what is called "slang". It is uncouth and unkind, the language of the back-street corner, the speech of the back street guttersnipes and the gutter press. We would call that the lowest level. Between the upper level of the first and the lowest level of the second there is a great gulf fixed. What is food and drink to one is poison to the other and what is poison to one is food and drink to the other.

There is, however, another level. It is the language of the vast majority of the populace. It is the language of the church, the school, the study, the home, the parlour, the shop, the business and the press.

We would call that the middle level. It has little to do with the peculiarities and distinctiveness of either of the other two levels. It is not a slave to where a man lives his life and does his business. What is important, however, is that those of the other two can both meet here.

It has been said that the essays of Lord Macauley move on the upper level. Those of much of our present day fiction move on the lowest level. Dickens, however, moves on the middle level and as is known, those from both the upper and lowest levels can understand and enter into the spirit of his narratives. In other words, it can be colloquial.

Now the languages in which the Bible was written, the Hebrew of the Old Testament and the Greek of the New Testament were not literary languages but the languages of the street, the market, the fields and the councils.

> *The Hebrew is almost our only example of the tongue at its period, but it is not a literary language in any case. The Greek of the New Testament is not the Eolic, the language of the lyrics of Sappho; nor the Doric, the language of war-songs or the chorus in the drama; nor the Ionic, the dialect of epic poetry; but the Attic Greek, and a corrupted form of that, a form corrupted by use in the streets and in the markets.*
>
> - Dr. McAfee, p 88

The origin of the languages of the Bible were colloquial.

This, of course, does not determine at what level the Bible is translated. Attempts have been made to put the Bible translation on to the upper level. On the other hand, attempts have been made by translation to put the Bible on the lower level. There are what are called elegant translations and there are those cast in slang language - the lowest level. The Authorized Version is on the middle level. Its language is in the middle English. It blends the exaltedness of the upper level with the popularity of the lowest.

The Authorized Version was aimed at being a Bible for all the people. It spawned a middle language which bridged the king and all his subjects.

Many of those who had translated the Scripture thought only of reaching a limited constituency. It was Tyndale who had his eyes on the total masses of the people. He believed that the Bible was the Book of God for all peoples.

The Authorized Version is not in the peculiar language of its time. The peculiar language of its time can be discovered in the translators' dedication to the king and in their preface to the reader.

What a difference between this language and that of the translation itself!

The language of the translation itself had lived from Wycliffe's translation through all the other successive versions into common use. Henry Hallam, the historian of the Constitution of England, accepts that. He states:

> *"The style of this translation is in general so enthusiastically praised, that no one is permitted either to qualify or even explain the grounds of his approbation. It is held to be the perfection of our English language. I shall not dispute this proposition; but one remark as to a matter of fact cannot reasonably be censured, that, in consequence of the principle of adherence to the original versions which had been kept up ever since the time of Henry VIII, it is not the language of the reign of James I. It may, in the eyes of many, be a better English, but it is not the English of Daniel Defoe, or Raleigh, or Bacon, as anyone may easily perceive."*
>
> - History of the Literature of Europe Vol 1 p 366

So the Authorized Version finally minted and consolidated an English of its own. It was not a matter of its language coming up to standard, but rather its language actually became the standard. It was itself the well of the Anglo Saxon tongue, pure and undefiled.

As Dr McAfee states:

> *"But it is true that the English of the King James version is not that of the time of James I, only because it is the English of history of the*

language. It has not immortalised for us the tongue of its times, because it has taken that tongue from its beginning and determined its form. It carefully avoided words that were counted coarse. On the other hand, it did not commit itself to words which were simply refinements of verbal construction. That, I say, is a general fact.

It can be illustrated in one or two ways. For instance, a word which has become common to us is the neuter possessive pronoun "its". That word does not occur in the editon of 1611, and appears first in an edition in the printing of 1660. In place of it, in the edition of 1611, the more dignified personal "his" or "her" is always used, and it continues for the most part in our familiar version. In this verse you notice it: "Look not upon the wine when it is red; when it giveth his colour aright in the cup." In the Levitical law especially, where reference is made to sacrifices, to the articles of the furniture of the tabernacle, or other neuter objects, the masculine pronoun is almost invariably used. In the original it was invariably used. You see the other form in the familiar verse about charity, that it "doth not behave itself unseemly, seeketh not her own, is not easily provoked." Now there is evidence that the neuter possessive pronoun was just coming into use. Shakespeare uses it ten times in his works, but ten times only, and a number of writers do not use it at all. It was, to be sure, a word beginning to be heard on the street, and for the most part on the lower level. The King James translators never used it. The dignified word was that masculine or feminine pronoun, and they always use it in place of the neuter.

On the other hand, there was a word which was coming into use on the upper level which has become common property to us now. It is the word "anxiety". It is not certain just when it came into use. I believe Shakespeare does not use it; and it occurs very little in the literature of the times. Probably it was known to these translators. When they came, however, to translating a word which now we translate by "anxious" or "anxiety" they did not use that word. It was not familiar. They used instead the word which represented the idea for the people of the middle level; they used the word "thought". So they said, "Take no thought for the morrow," where we would say, "Be not anxious for the morrow." There is a contemporary document which illustrates how that word "thought" was commonly used, in which we read: "In five hundred years only two queens died in child birth, Queen Catherine Parr having died rather of thought." That was written about the time of the King James version, and "thought" evidently means worry or anxiety. Neither of those words, the neuter possessive pronoun or the new word "anxious" got into the King James version. One was coming into proper use from the lower level, and one was coming into proper use from the upper level. They had not yet so arrived that they could be used.

One result of this care to preserve dignity and also popularity appears in the fact that so few words of the English version have become obsolete. Words disappear upward out of the upper level or downward out of the lower level, but it takes a long time for a word to get out of a language once it is in confirmed use on the middle level. Of course, the version itself has tended to keep words familiar; but no book, no matter how widely used, can prevent some words from passing off the stage or from changing their meaning so noticeably that they are virtually different words. Yet even in those words which do not become common there is very little tendency to obsolescence in the King James version. More words of Shakespeare have become obsolete or have changed their meaning than in the King James version."

- pp 84,85,86,87

So high is the English language standard of the 1611 Authorized Version that the committee appointed by the Upper House of the Province of Canterbury of the Church of England on February 10th, 1870 to report on the desirability of a revision of the Authorized Version, stated in their report submitted in May of the same year:-

"WE DO NOT CONTEMPLATE ANY NEW TRANSLATION OF THE BIBLE, OR ANY ALTERATION OF THE LANGUAGE, EXCEPT WHERE, IN

THE JUDGMENT OF THE MOST COMPETENT OF SCHOLARS, SUCH CHANGE IS NECESSARY ... THAT IN SUCH CHANGES THE STYLE OF THE LANGUAGE IN THE EXISTING (AV) VERSION BE CLOSELY FOLLOWED."

Could we have a greater witness than that after over 250 years the English of the Authorized Version stood the test?

Professor Albert Cooke of Yale University said, "The movement of English diction which in the seventeenth and eighteenth centuries was on the whole away from the Bible, now returns with ever-accelerating speed towards it."

Professor Cooke wrote *The Authorized Version of the Bible and its Influence* as a chapter for the Fourth Volume of *The Cambridge History of English Literature*. He states:

The theme or themes of the Bible are of the utmost comprehensiveness, depth and poignancy of appeal. In the treatment there is nowhere a trace of levity or insincerity to be detected. The heart of a man is felt to be pulsating behind every line. There is no straining for effect, no obtrusive ornament, no complacent parading of the devices of art. Great matters are presented with warmth of sentiment, in a simple style; and nothing is more likely to render literature enduring.

Another trait of good literature exemplified by the Bible is breadth. Take, for example, the story of Jacob, the parable of the Prodigal Son, or St Paul's speech on Mars hill. Only the essentials are given. There is no petty and befogging detail. The characters, the events, or the arguments stand out with clearness, even with boldness. An inclusive and central effect is produced with a few masterly strokes, so that the resulting impression is one of conciseness and economy.

Closely associated with this quality of breadth is that of vigour. The authors of the Bible have no time nor mind to spend upon the elaboration of curiosities, or upon minute and trifling points. Every sentence, nay, every word, must count. The spirit which animates the whole must inform every particle. There is no room for delicate shadings; the issues are too momentous, the concerns too pressing, to admit of introducing anything that can be spared. A volume is compressed into a page, a page into a line.

And God said, Let there be light, and there was light
Jesus wept.

It would not be difficult to show how all these qualities flow necessarily from the intense preoccupation of the Biblical authors with matters affecting all they held dear, all their hopes and fears with respect to their country, their family and themselves, at the present and in a boundless future. Even when the phrases employed seem cool and measured, they represent a compressed energy like that of a tightly coiled spring, tending to actuate effort and struggle of many kinds, and to open out into arts and civilisations of which the Hebrew never dreamed.

- pp 29,30

Cooke goes on:

The influences which moulded the English language into a proper vehicle for so stupendous a literary creation as the English Bible must next be briefly considered ... Throughout the Old English period, most of the literature produced was strongly coloured by biblical diction. Even a work like Bede's Ecclesiastical History of the English People was under this influence. By about the year 1000, the language was able to render the Latin of Jerome ... according to the computations of Marsh, about 93 per cent of the words of the Authorized Version, counting repetitions of the same word, are native English (pp. 35-37).

Cooke then states that four traits in the original Scriptures make them easy to translate into all languages.

One, *universality of interest*. There are words in all languages which express that about which all men talk.

Two, *concreteness and picturesqueness of their language* avoiding abstractness which would make it difficult to translate.

Three, *the simplicity of its structure.*

Four, *the rhythm so that part follows part* catching a swing which is not difficult to imitate.

Because of the diligence of the Authorized Version translators the universality of interest, the concreteness and picturesqueness, the simplicity and the rhythm of the Original Scriptures have been captivated.

That is what has made our English Authorized Version what it is, a classic for more languages than any other book.

Cooke says:

Among the qualifications of a good translator, the first, undoubtedly, is that he shall be penetrated by a sense of the surpassing value of his original, and a corresponding sense of the importance of his task. This will preserve him from flippancy and meanness, by imbuing him with earnestness and humility. It will make him ready to follow wherever he is led by the text, and will prevent him from preening himself upon prettiness of phrase, or any fancies of his own. Such a translator will strive with all his might after fidelity to word and sense, and after the utmost clearness and simplicity of rendering, avoiding, on the one hand, the trivial, and on the other, the ornate or pompous. He will conform to the genius of his own tongue while endeavouring to transfer to it the treasures of another; and, besides possessing naturally, he will cultivate, in every proper way, a high sensitiveness to that music of the phrase, which, in the case of the Bible, is but another name for the music of the heart.

- pp 35,36

The vocabulary of the English Bible is by no means extensive.

Shakespeare used from 15,000 to 20,000 words. Milton in his versification uses 13,000.

In the Hebrew Old Testament there are 5,642 words and in the Greek New Testament 4,800. However in the whole Authorized Version there are only about 6,000 different words. The vocabulary is narrow - one third of Shakespeare's vocabulary to record the very Word of God.

These words are all short words. The average Bible word is barely over four letters. Taking out the longer proper names the average would be under four letters.

Addison, commenting on this fact, said:

> *If anyone would judge of the beauties of poetry that are to be met with the divine writings, and examine how kindly the Hebrew manners of speech mix and incorporate with the English language, after having perused the Book of Psalms, let him read a literal translation of Horace of Pindar. He will find in these two last such an absurdity and confusion of style with such a comparative poverty of imagination, as will make him very sensible of what I have been here advancing.*

- McAfee p 107

To illustrate, look at the Ten Commandments in Exodus chapter 20.

There are 319 words in all. 250 of these words are one syllable and 60 are of two syllables or over. In the Sermon on the Mount 82 percent of all the words in our Authorized Version are words of one syllable.

Short words are strong and clear. The strength of our English Bible lies in such clear-cut wording.

The story is told of a very powerful preacher who preached a most eloquent and elegant sermon on Creation. When he concluded his pulpit oratory he said to an old listener, "What do you think of that?" The old listener replied, "You can't beat Moses!" Certainly, you can't beat the Bible! It goes straight to the point with the clear-cut sharpness of a rapier blade.

THE FACT IS THE LANGUAGE OF THE AUTHORIZED VERSION (KJV) OF THE ENGLISH BIBLE IS UNSURPASSABLY PRE-EMINENT BEING THE FIRST FROM THE WELL UNDEFILED AND INDEED THE VERY WELL ITSELF.

6 The foundation of the English Authorised Version (KJV) of the Holy Bible is unsurpassably pre-eminent in
majesty, chastity and eternity

Professor Cooke, already referred to, says:

The greatest of all translations is the English Bible. It is even more than that: it is the greatest of English books, the first of English classics, the source of the greatest influence upon English character and speech. Apart from any questions of dogma and theology, the Bible has all the marks of a classic. Its themes are those of perpetual concern in great literature: God, Man and the Universe. It has, in spite of its vast diversity, a supreme unity.

When we think of the high repute in which the Authorized Version is held by men of learning and renown, we must remember, too, that in a special sense it has been the great book of the poor and unlettered. The one book that every household was sure to possess was the Bible; and it was read, sometimes ignorantly, sometimes unwisely, but always memorably. To many a poor man the English Bible has been a university, the kindly mother from whom he has drawn history, philosophy and a way of great speech. The modern world has seen many changes; but it has, so far, seen no movement that has shaken the supremacy of the greatest of English books. If ever the Bible falls from its high sovereignty, we may be sure that the English character has fallen with it.

- pp 178 and 180

Alas! Alas! We are seeing that today.

The Bible is the Word of God. It is also the Book of God's people. Rabbie Burns, Scotland's national bard, knew this when he wrote his "Cotter's Saturday Night". In two stanzas of that beautiful descriptive poem he presents the two great aspects of the English Bible; its messages to the soul and conscience, and its indestructible literary quality. Take them in this order:

The cheerfu' supper done, wi' serious face,
They, round the ingle, form a circle wide;
The sire turns o'er with patriarchal grace,
The big ha' Bible, ance his father's pride:
His bonnet reverently is laid aside,
His lyart haffets wearing thin and bare;
Those strains that once did sweet in Zion glide,
He wales a portion with judicious care;
And "Let us worship God," he says, with solemn air.

The priest-like father reads the sacred page,
How Abram was the friend of God on high;
Or Moses bade eternae warfare rage
With Amalek's ungracious progeny;
Or how the royal bard did groaning lie
Beneath the stroke of Heaven's avenging ire;
Or Job's pathetic plaint and wailing cry;
Or rapt Isaiah's wild seraphic fire;
Or other holy seers that tune the sacred lyre.

Sir Arthur Quiller Cough, lecturing at Cambridge on "Reading the Bible," has placed before his students a few great sentences like these:

Thine eyes shall see the King in his beauty: they shall behold the land that is very far off.

And a man shall be as an hiding place from the wind, and a covert from the tempest; as rivers of water in a dry place and as the shadow of a great rock in a weary land.

So when this corruptible shall have put on incorruption, and this mortal shall have put on immortality ...

Then he says:

"When a nation has achieved this manner of diction, these rhythms for its dearest beliefs, a literature is surely established ... The Authorized Version set a seal on our national style ... It has cadences homely and sublime, yet so harmonises them that the voice is always one. Simple men - holy men of heart like Izaak Walton and Bunyan - have their lips touched and speak to the homelier tune."

Bunyan derived his thought and his style from the English Bible. And Bunyan's Grace Abounding and his Pilgrim's Progress lead us back to this well of homely religion and English undefiled. Bunyan knew the Authorised Version of the English Bible as perhaps no other man has known it. Its language became his breath. In passage after passage of The Pilgrim's Progress we seem to be reading the Bible through the medium of his own words. Take these words of Mr Greatheart in the Valley of the Shadow:

"This is like doing business in great waters, or like going down into the deep; this is like being in the heart of the Sea, and like going down to the Bottoms of the Mountains: Now it seems as if the Earth with its bars were about us for ever. But let them that walk in darkness and have no light, trust in the name of the Lord, and stay upon their God. For my part, as I have told you already, I have gone often through this Valley, and have been much harder put to it than now I am, and yet you see I am alive. I would not boast, for that I am not mine own Saviour. But I trust we shall have a good deliverance. Come let us pray for light to Him that can lighten our darkness, and that can rebuke, not only these, but all the Satans in Hell."

The language of the Bible shaped the speech of England, and Bunyan learned to use that language better than anyone else. In The Pilgrim's Progress the common people found no word or sentence they did not understand.

The Professor of English Literature in Cambridge University continues:

"Proud men, scholars - Milton, Sir Thomas Browne - practice the rolling Latin sentence, but upon the rhythms of the Bible, they too, fall back ... (tributes to the Authorized Version).

The precise man Addison cannot excel one parable in brevity or in heavenly clarity: the two parts of Johnson's antithesis come to no more than this, "Our Lord has gone up to the sound of a trumpet; with the sound of a trump our Lord has gone up." The Bible controls its enemy Gibbon as surely as it haunts the curious music of a light sentence of Thackeray's. It is in everything we see, hear, feel, because it is in us, in our blood".

Coleridge said that it "will keep any man from being vulgar in point of style." Assuredly it kept the Bedford tinker from being vulgar, and hardly less Daniel Defoe. The Bible profoundly influenced Ruskin's style. "It is ingrained," says his biographer, "in the texture of almost every piece from his pen." Macaulay refers to our Bible as "a book which, if everything else in our language should perish, would alone suffice to show the whole extent of its beauty and power." Milton declared: "There are no songs comparable to the songs of Zion, no orations equal to those of the prophets." Landor wrote to a friend: "I am heartily glad to witness your veneration for a book which, to say nothing of its holiness or authority, contains more specimens of genius and taste than any other volume in existence." And Hobbes had the literary study of the Bible in mind when he shrewdly wrote in "Leviathan": "It is not the bare words but the scope of the writer that giveth the true light by which any writing is to be interpreted; and they that insist upon single texts, without considering the main design, can derive nothing from them clearly: but rather by casting atoms of Scripture as dust before men's eyes, make everything more obscure than it is."

It has sometimes been asked whether the Authorized Version of 1604-11 could have been done without the aid of men of letters, and even one or more poets. How could the cadences of the Psalms, the sublime questions and answers of the Book of Job, the rhapsodies of Isaiah, and the eloquence of Paul at Athens have been rendered by forty-seven scholars of whom not one has left his mark on literature? The extraordinary suggestion has been made that Shakespeare who, in 1604, was at the height of his genius, may have been called in to give poetry and majesty to our Bible.

- Outline of Literature pp. 77,78,79

Forty-seven scholars! Yet, not one of them left their mark on literature! It was the Book, however, which they did not write but which they faithfully translated which left its unerasable broad mark on all living.

That Book did not require an injection of Shakespeare's poetry or majesty.

It had a poetry which relegated some of Shakespeare's lines to the place of doggerel. It had a majesty which banished Shakespeare's gilding to utter ignominy and shame.

That Book had the Majesty of all majesties, the Chastity of all chastities and the Eternity of all eternities. Its Majesty is the Gloriousness of God. Its Chastity is the Holiness of God. Its Eternity is the Agelessness of God.

Here is one example of its Majesty revealing the Gloriousness of God:

"The Lord is my strength and song, and he is become my salvation: he is my God, and I will prepare him an habitation; my father's God, and I will exalt him. The Lord is a man of war: the Lord is his name. Pharaoh's chariots and his hosts hath he cast into the sea: his chosen captains also are drowned in the Red sea. The depths have covered them: they sank into the bottom as a stone. Thy right hand, O Lord, is become glorious in power: thy right hand, O Lord, hath dashed in pieces the enemy. And in the greatness of thine excellency thou hast

overthrown them that rose up against thee: thou sentest forth thy words, which consumed them as stubble ... Thou didst blow with thy wind, the sea covered them: they sank as lead in the mighty waters. Who is like unto thee, O Lord, among the gods? who is like thee, glorious in holiness, fearful in praises, doing wonders?"

- Exodus 15: 2-7, 10-11

Here is an example of its Chastity revealing the Holiness of God:

"Have mercy upon me, O God, according to thy lovingkindness: according unto the multitude of thy tender mercies blot out my transgressions. Wash me throughly from mine iniquity, and cleanse me from my sin. For I acknowledge my transgressions: and my sin is ever before me. Against thee, thee only, have I sinned, and done this evil in thy sight: that thou mightest be justified when thou speakest, and be clear when thou judgest. Behold, I was shapen in iniquity; and in sin did my mother conceive me. Behold, thou desirest truth in the inward parts: and in the hidden part thou shalt make me to know wisdom. Purge me with hyssop, and I shall be clean: wash me, and I shall be whiter than snow. Make me to hear joy and gladness; that the bones which thou hast broken may rejoice. Hide thy face from my sins, and blot out all mine iniquities. Create in me a clean heart, O God: and renew a right spirit within me. Cast me not away from thy presence; and take not thy holy spirit from me. Restore unto me the joy of thy salvation; and uphold me with thy free spirit. Then will I teach transgressors thy ways; and sinners shall be converted unto thee. Deliver me from blood-guiltiness, O God, thou God of my salvation: and my tongue shall sing aloud of thy righteousness. O Lord, open thou my lips; and my mouth shall shew forth thy praise. For thou desirest not sacrifice; else would I give it: thou delightest not in burnt offering. The sacrifices of God are a broken spirit: a broken and a contrite heart, O God, thou wilt not despise. Do good in thy good pleasure unto Zion: build thou the walls of Jerusalem. Then shalt thou be pleased with the sacrifices of righteousness, with burnt offering and whole burnt offering: then shall they offer bullocks upon thine altar"

- Psalm 51

Herein is an example of its Eternity revealing the Agelessness of God:

"I said, O my God, take me not away in the midst of my days: thy years are throughout all generations,. Of old hast thou laid the foundation of the earth: and the heavens are the work of thy hands. They shall perish but thou shalt endure: yea, all of them shall wax old like a garment; as a vesture shalt thou change them, and they shall be changed: But thou art the same, and thy years shall have no end"

- Psalm 102: 24-27

Truly never Book spake like the Bible. God breathed into this Book and it became living Scripture to the English reader.

Its undimmed glory, its untarnishable chastity and its unending eternity demonstrate that it is the Word of God in the English tongue.

C S Lewis was right when he wrote in the Literary Impact of the Authorised Version:

There is ... no possibility of considering the literary impact of the Authorized Version apart from that of the Bible in general. The Authorized Verison owes to the original its matter, its images, and its figures.

Solomon Caesar Malan, Vicar of Broadminister, in his *Vindication of the Authorized Version* states:

... it stands pre-eminent when side by side with more modern versions, not only for its devout adherence to the original texts, but also for the beauty of its style ... *So true is this, that whereas neighbouring nations have had, within a short period, a succession of versions of the Bible in their respective languages, to the detriment of union and of uniformity among the readers of the Bible in those countries, the English Version has stood on its own merits, and has shone of its own lustre for nearly two centuries and a half.*

Thus it is that it has entered into the very substance of the nation, It is interwoven with its sinews, and forms more than any other book ever did - an unseen, by many perhaps, unacknowledged, or even neglected, but still a living element in the prosperity of the people ... **THESE LASTING AND WHOLESOME EFFECTS ARE THE RESULT OF THE ENGLISH BIBLE BEING ONE AND THE SAME FOR ALL. IF, INSTEAD OF ONLY ONE BIBLE, ENGLAND HAD, LIKE SOME OTHER COUNTRIES, MANY BIBLES, THAT VARIETY ALONE WOULD BREED AND FOSTER ENDLESS DIVISION...**

Their reverence for the Sacred Scriptures induced them [KJV translators] to be as literal as they could to avoid obscurity; and it must be acknowledged that they were extremely happy in the simplicity and dignity of their expressions. Their adherence to the Hebrew idiom is supposed at once to have enriched and adorned our language; and, as they laboured for the general benefit of the learned and the unlearned, they avoided all words of Latin origin when they could find words in their own language ...

Thus, then, the English Bible has not only stood for centuries, and **NOW STANDS ON ITS OWN MERITS AS A TRUE WITNESS OF THE INSPIRED TEXT OF SCRIPTURE**; *but it is also strong of its own strength, in being, as the highest authorities tell us, "the best standard of the English language" ...* **For "our translators," says Dr Adam Clarke, "not only made a standard translation, but they have made their translation the standard of our language. THE ENGLISH TONGUE, IN THEIR DAY, WAS NOT EQUAL TO SUCH A WORK; BUT GOD ENABLED THEM TO STAND AS UPON MOUNT SINAI, AND CRANE UP THEIR COUNTRY'S LANGUAGE TO THE DIGNITY OF THE ORIGINALS,** *so that after the lapse of two hundred and fifty years, the English Bible is, with very few exceptions, the standard of the purity and excellence of the English tongue. The original, from which it was taken, is alone superior to the Bible translated by the authority of King James."*

Such considerations, however, have no weight with many who are willing to sacrifice much to the love of change; or at all events, who seem to take pleasure in aiming blows at everything that is of yesterday. **Everything now must keep pace with the age; even the word of God** ... *And yet wisdom neither came with us, nor will die with us, As regards the Authorized Version then, and those who find fault with it, "let us not too hastily conclude," says Mr Whittaker, "that the translators have fallen on evil days and evil tongues, because* **it has occasionally happened that an individual, as inferior to them in erudition as in talents and integrity, is found questioning their motives, or denying their qualifications for the task which they so well performed** ... **It [the KJV] may be compared with any translation in the world, without fear or inferiority; it has not shrunk from the most rigorous examination; it challenges investigation;** *and, in spite of numerous `attempts to supersede it, it has hitherto remained unrivalled in the affections of the country."*

And God grant it may long continue so, for the good of the people to which it belongs!

I purpose therefore ... to look into the charges thus brought forward against the English Bible, with those who cling to it as they ought, affectionately and devoutly; in order to assist them in expelling from their mind all doubt on the subject. Meanwhile, **they may rest assured that, hitherto, all attempts at improvement upon their Bible have come far short of it in language, in style, in truthfulness, and above all, in a generally correct and devout rendering of the original text** (Malan, A Vindication, pp. i-xvi, xxii-xxvi).

... we now hear from many, that the English Bible is no longer suited to the exigencies of the present day, but that our advanced state of knowledge loudly calls for a new revision. An evil day that will be when it comes. However, Bishop Middleton holds out no encouragement to them when he says: **"The style of our present version is incomparably superior to anything which might be expected from the financial and perverted taste of our own age.** *It is simple, it is harmonious, it is energetic; and, which is of no small*

importance, use has made it familiar, and time has rendered it sacred" ... its words are "household words," ... its simple and hallowed language is understood and loved alike, by the poor peasant and by the august Sovereign, whom it binds to her people. **England has not "a Bible," one of many to choose from, like her neighbours; but "the Bible" is in every English home; and "my Bible" in English, means that one Book the very words of which are the same for all**" (Malan, A Vindication, pp. xviii, xix).

Who will be bold, or I might almost say hardened enough, if not perhaps to pull down, yet even to whitewash the stately edifice of the English Bible? ... It might possibly be better adapted to the fastidious taste of the age; but then, unbroken associations of two centuries and a half, together with much of national individuality, would perish for ever and those persons who think the Authorized Version antiquated would be the first to regret the change ... For independently of the words of the Bible being sacred in all languages, the language of the English Bible in particular is consecrated ... the vernacular translation of the Bible has formed and fixed the language of the country" (Malan, A Vindication of the Authorized Version, 1856, pp. 111, iv, xiv).

HS Millar, though a supporter of the Westcott Hort Text and the Revised Version, had to admit:

For more than three centuries the King James Version has been the Bible of the English-speaking world, and there does not seem to be much abatement, even in favour of the Revised Version. More copies are being sold each year. Its simple, majestic, Anglo-Saxon tongue, its clear, sparkling style, its directness and force of utterance, have made it the model in language, style and dignity of some of the choicest writers of the last two centuries. Added to the above characteristics, its reverential and spiritual tone and attitude have made it the life of the Christian church, for its own words have been regarded as authoritative and binding. It has endeared itself to the hearts and lives of millions of Christians and has molded the characters of the

My plea for *the Old Sword*   69

leaders in every walk of life in the greatest nation of the world. During all these centuries, King James' Version has become a vital part of the English-speaking world, socially, morally, religiously, and politically. Launched with the endorsement of the regal and scholarly authority of the seventeenth century, its conquest and rule have been supreme

> - HS Miller, General Biblical Introduction, pp. 356,66; Miller quotes part of this paragraph from Ira Price's The Ancestry of our English Bible

Read these three portions from the Holy Book. One is oratorical, the second is exhortatory and the third narratory. Isaiah chapter thirty-five:

The wilderness and the solitary place shall be glad for them; and the desert shall rejoice, and blossom as the rose. It shall blossom abundantly, and rejoice even with joy and singing: the glory of Lebanon shall be given unto it, the excellency of Carmel and Sharon, they shall see the glory of the Lord, and the excellency of our God. Strengthen ye the weak hands, and confirm the feeble knees. Say to them that are of a fearful heart, Be strong, fear not: behold, your God will come with vengeance, even God with a recompence; he will come and save you. Then the eyes of the blind shall be opened, and the ears of the deaf shall be unstopped. Then shall the lame man leap as an hart, and the tongue of the dumb sing: for in the wilderness shall waters break out, and streams in the desert. And the parched ground shall become a pool, and the thirsty land springs of water: in the habitation of dragons, where each lay, shall be grass with reeds and rushes. And an highway shall be there, and a way, and it shall be called The way of holiness; the unclean shall not pass over it; but it shall be for those: the wayfaring men, though fools, shall not err therein. No lion shall be there, nor any ravenous beast shall go up thereon, it shall not be found there; but the redeemed shall walk there: And the ransomed of the Lord shall return, and come to Zion with songs and everlasting joy upon their heads; they shall obtain joy and gladness, and sorrow and sighing shall flee away.

The Acts of the Apostles, chapter twenty verses 17-38:

And from Miletus he sent to Ephesus, and called the elders of the church. And when they were come to him, he said unto them, Ye know, from the first day that I came into Asia, after what manner I have been with you at all seasons. Serving the Lord with all humility of mind, and with many tears, and temptations, which befell me by the lying in wait of the Jews: And how I kept back nothing that was profitable unto you, but have shewed you, and have taught you publickly, and from house to house. Testifying both to the Jews, and also to the Greeks, repentance toward God, and faith toward our Lord Jesus Christ. And now, behold, I go bound in the spirit unto Jerusalem, not knowing the things that shall befall me there: Save that the Holy Ghost witnesseth in every city, saying that bonds and afflictions abide me. But none of these things move me, neither count I my life dear unto myself, so that I might finish my course with joy, and the ministry, which I have received of the Lord Jesus, to testify the gospel of the grace of God. And now, behold, I know that ye all, among whom I have gone preaching the kingdom of God, shall see my face no more. Wherefore I take you to record this day that I am pure from the blood of all men. For I have not shunned to declare unto you all the counsel of God. Take heed therefore unto yourselves, and to all the flock, over the which the Holy Ghost hath made you overseers, to feed the church of God, which he hath purchased with his own blood, For I know this, that after my departing shall grievous wolves enter in among you, not sparing the flock. Also of your own selves shall men arise, speaking perverse things, to draw away disciples after them. Therefore watch, and remember, that by the space of three years I ceased not to warn every one night and day with tears. And now, brethren, I commend you to God, and to the word of his grace, which is able to build you up, and to give you an inheritance among all them which are sanctified. I have coveted no man's silver, or gold, or apparel. Yea, ye yourselves know, that these hands have ministered unto my necessities, and to them that were with me. I have shewed you all things, how that so labouring ye ought to support the weak, and to remember the words of the Lord Jesus, how he said, It is more blessed to give than to receive. And when he had thus spoken he kneeled down, and prayed with them all. And they all wept sore, and fell on Paul's neck, and kissed him. Sorrowing most of all for the words which he spake, that they should see his face no more. And they accompanied him unto the ship.

Luke chapter twenty-four verses 13-35:

And, behold, two of them went that same day to a village called Emmaus, which was from Jerusalem about threescore furlongs. And they talked together of all these things which had happened. And it came to pass, that while they communed together and reasoned, Jesus himself drew near, and went with them. But their eyes were holden that they should not know him. And he said unto them, What manner of communications are these that ye have one to another, as ye walk, and are sad? And one of them, whose name was Cleopas, answering said unto him, Art thou only a stranger in Jerusalem, and hast not known the things which are come to pass there in these days? And he said unto them, What things? And they said unto him, Concerning Jesus of Nazareth, which was a prophet mighty in deed and word before God and all the people: And how the chief priests and our rulers delivered him to be condemned to death, and have crucified him. But we trusted that it had been he which should have redeemed Israel: and beside all this, to day is the third day since these things were done. Yea, and certain women also of our company made us astonished, which were early at the sepulchre; and when they found not his body, they came, saying, that they had also seen a vision of angels, which said that he was alive. And certain of them which were with us went to the sepulchre, and found it even so as the women had said: but him they saw not. Then he said unto them, O fools, and slow of heart to believe all that the prophets have spoken: Ought not Christ to have suffered these things, and to enter into his glory? And beginning at Moses and all the prophets, he expounded unto them in all the scriptures the things concerning himself. And they drew nigh unto the village, whither they went: and he made as though he would have gone further. But they constrained him, saying, Abide with us: for it is toward evening and the day is far spent. And he went in to tarry with them. And it came to pass, as he sat at meat with them, he took bread, and blessed it, and brake, and gave to them. And their eyes were opened, and they knew him; and he vanished out of their sight. And they said one to another, Did not our hearts burn within us, while he talked with us by the way, and while he opened to us the scriptures? And they rose up the same hour and returned to Jerusalem, and found the eleven gathered together, and them that were with them. Saying, The Lord is risen indeed, and hath appeared to Simon. And they told what things were done in the way, and how he was known of them in breaking of bread.

THE FACT IS THAT THE SPEECH OF THE AUTHORIZED VERSION (KJV) OF THE ENGLISH BIBLE IS UNSURPASSABLY PRE-EMINENT IN MAJESTY, CHASTITY AND ETERNITY.

7 The doctrine of the English Authorised Version (KJV) of the Holy Bible is unsurpassably pre-eminent
being couched in sound words in keeping with unwavering belief in the revealed truths of the Word of God

Paul exhorted "the holding fast of sound words", and in the doctrinal realm the Authorized Version is pre-eminent in doing just that.

The Holy Word itself poses the question - If the foundations be destroyed what can the righteous do? - Psalm 11:33.

The blunt answer is they cannot do at all, they are undone.

Those modern English versions which claim to be the scholarly and sound versions which we should use, and discard the Authorized Version, have certainly destroyed the doctrinal foundation of the faith once delivered to the saints.

The Westminster Confession of Faith is a statement of the Historical Christian Faith founded on and grounded on the Bible, and sets forth the Faith common to Protestants.

The Confession, though Presbyterian in origin, was based on Archbishop Usher's *Articles of Religion of the Episcopal Irish Church* and was adapted, except in matters of Church polity and the sacraments, by the Congregationalists in their Savoy Confession and by the Baptists in their London Confession. So it represents a common Christian doctrinal system which all these bodies understood the Scriptures taught.

All the great doctrines defined in these confessions have a galaxy of proof texts referred to upon which each doctrine is founded. The supreme test with them was that of the prophet Isaiah "To the law and to the testimony, if they speak not according to this word it is because there is no light in them" (Isaiah 8:20).

Notice that all these modern Bibles claim the definite "New" as their common title - The New English Bible, The New International Version, The New King James Version, The New American Version.

The old foundations must go under the bulldozer of the "new".

In the modern English versions there is the tendency to dilute the great doctrines of the Biblical Revelation by deleting the use of sound words which define those doctrines or by deleting them out of the Scriptures altogether.

Let me take the "super-star" version, the New International Version (NIV), a version widely used by "evangelicals" so-called. It dilutes the cardinal doctrines of the Bible and in some cases deletes them altogether.

Let us take a few examples.

THE INSPIRATION OF THE BIBLE

The Inspiration of the Bible is a cardinal doctrine of Holy Scripture. It is all important as it sets forth the Bible as the only infallible rule of faith and practice.

Now the NIV deletes the very word "inspiration" from the foundational proof text quoted in the Westminster Confession of Faith (WCF) as revealing this doctrine.

II Timothy 3:16 *"All scripture is given by inspiration of God,"* proof text, chapter one WCF. The NIV deletes the word *inspiration* from the text altogether and substitutes *"God breathed"*. The other reference to inspiration in the Bible is in Job 32:8 *"The inspiration of the Almighty giveth them understanding"*. Again the word *inspiration* is jettisoned altogether by the NIV and the word *"breath"* substituted. This again leads to a diluting, to an undermining, to a corroding of a great cardinality, removing the word *inspiration* from the Bible.

Take another text quoted in the Confession of Faith as proof of the certainty of the truth of God's Word - the inerrancy of Holy Scripture. Proverbs 22:19-21 *"Have I not written unto thee excellent things"* verse 20. *"That I might make thee know the certainty of the words of truth"* verse 21. Proof texts for chapter one WCF. The NIV changes *"excellent things"* into *thirty sayings* and the *"certainty of the words of truth"* diluted into *"true and reliable sayings"*. This overall tendency of watering down is manifested across the pages of the NIV.

Those who use the Authorized Version are looked down upon by the apologists for the NIV as ignoramuses, who do not understand the Hebrew and the Greek and therefore are in no position to judge. Unable to answer the arguments of the defenders of the Authorized Version, they turn to pouring scorn on their scholarship or lack of scholarship.

In reality their argument is blatantly false for they are really affirming that all who use the NIV have the scholarship to make the right judgment.

Let us get the matter right. The Bible is not the production of man but the product of God. It is the Word of God. It was not delivered unto the scholars - Greek, Hebrew or otherwise, but to the saints. *"The faith which was once delivered to the saints"* Jude 3.

God has delivered His Book to the custody, not of the scholars, the universities, colleges or seats of learning, but only to His saints.

Can any ordinary saint who has no knowledge whatever of the original languages know what is a proper version of God's Word or which is absolutely reliable? The answer is "yes" or else Jude verse 3 is error. Jude verse 3 is not error but divinely revealed truth.

The attempt to bamboozle the ordinary saints of God with irrelevant controversy must be demonstrated. The ploy to take from the saints their divinely appointed role of custody of the Book and place it in the hands of scholars must be exposed for what it is, a device of the devil himself.

Thank God for the simplicity which is in Christ which devastates the duplicity which is in Satan.

But how can the saint know?

The answer is as plain as the midday sun - The saint knows the Author of the Book and has received what no amount of learning can impart - the divinely imparted gift of spiritual discernment.

"But the natural man receiveth not the things of the Spirit of God: for they are foolishness unto him: neither can he know them, because they are spiritually discerned" (I Corinthians 2:14).

In knowing God the saint knows two things -

One, that God does not lie and two, He cannot contradict Himself. It follows therefore that the Word of God cannot lie or contradict itself. It will be divinely consistent, for it is the Holy Word of the Thrice Holy God. Two, that the briefer statements of truth in the Bible can only be rightly explained by those fuller statements of the same Divine Author in the same Book speaking with the same Authority and thus setting His seal that He is true. *"Let God be true and every man a liar"* (Romans 3:4).

In other words, the Bible has the witness in itself. In this sense, the saint needs no man to teach him for he hath an unction from the Holy One and knoweth all things.

My plea for the Old Sword   77

"But ye have an unction from the Holy One, and ye know all things. But the anointing which ye have received of Him abideth in you, and ye need not that any man teach you: but as the same anointing teacheth you of all things, and is truth, and is no lie, and even as it hath taught you, ye shall abide in Him" (I John 2:20 and 27).

Someone has rightly said about the Word of God:

"The Bible, the Divine Book, having the witness in itself, is also the most human of all books, and comes forth in the midst of the earth, saying, 'Unto you, O men, I call, and my voice is to the sons of men; come unto me, know me, try me, prove me. I speak as to wise men - judge ye what I say. The Words that I speak unto you, they are spirit, and they are life; judge not according to appearance, but judge righteous judgment; to the Law and to the Testimony, adding nought thereto, and taking nought therefrom."

God calls His people to *"Try the spirits whether they are of God, because many false prophets are gone out into the world"* (I John 4:1). The great test is the acknowledgement that the Son of God and God the Son is come in the flesh, i.e. that God has incarnated Himself in the flesh. Let us then test the NIV by these incontestable principles, the principles of consistency, confirmation and confession.

I choose but one text for this purpose. Let us open the Bible at that book which commences with the words, *"The beginning of the Gospel"* (Mark 1:1) Where more appropriate to start than at the beginning?

AV1611	**NIV 1983**	**Notes in NIV**
Mark 1: 1-3	Mark 1:1-3	
The beginning of the gospel of Jesus Christ, the Son of God.	*The beginning of the gospel about Jesus Christ, the Son of God.a*	a. Some manuscripts do not have *the Son of God.*

AV1611	NIV 1983	Notes in NIV
As it is written in the prophets, Behold, I send my messenger before thy face, which shall prepare thy way before thee.	*It is written in Isaiah the prophet: "I will send my messenger ahead of you, who will prepare your way."b*	b. Malachi 3:1
The voice of one crying in the wilderness, Prepare ye the way of the Lord, make his paths straight.	*A voice of one calling in the desert, "Prepare the way for the Lord, make straight the paths for him."c*	c. Isaiah 40:3

Note carefully the Authorized Version is perfectly consistent with itself throughout these three verses. Its statements are direct, simple and straightforward. It has nothing in the margin demonstrating that the text could or should be corrected or has an alternative to be considered.

On the other hand the NIV is quite inconsistent with itself, incorrect in its statements, self-contradictory and on its showing, the Gospel of Jesus Christ is a mass of contradictions and at the best a cunningly devised fable.

In the Authorized Version the remarkable and consistent statement of verse one is supported and confirmed by two proof texts of evidence, which appear at length, and are extracts from the Prophets.

"As it is written in the prophets, Behold, I send my messenger before thy face, which shall prepare thy way before thee. The voice of one crying in the wilderness, Prepare ye the way of the Lord, make his paths straight" (Mark 1: 2-3).

The heart of the first verse is that Jesus Christ is the Son of God in the highest and strictest sense. This is consistent with the fuller confirmatory scriptures elsewhere in the Word of God.

In the NIV the verse is changed from *"the gospel of Jesus Christ,"* to, *"the gospel **about** Jesus Christ."* This is a fundamental change and changes Mark's gospel from being Christ's gospel to just a gospel **about** Christ. The verse is then completely undermined by the note, *"some manuscripts do not have the Son of God."* This strikes at the heart of the statement *"the Son of God"* which is the heart of verse one. This note haemorrhages away the life-blood of this revealed truth. If the translators give no credence to this omission why then do they record it? By putting it in they show that they are following a cunningly devised fable.

The saint knows that Jesus Christ is the Son of God and with spiritual discernment, and not requiring any knowledge whatever of the Greek language, rejects the fable of the perversion and acclaims the fact of the true version.

"If any man do His will, he shall know of the doctrine, whether it be of God, or whether I speak of myself" (John 7:17).

The NIV goes on to show that the heart of verse one, now emasculated by the footnote supporting the complete omission of the words *"the Son of God"* is supported by one proof only. The proof of two distinct prophesies has been truncated into one violent compression and the majestic name of Isaiah hung as a sign over the falsehood.

The saint of God, without any understanding of either the Hebrew language or the Greek, knows that the Word of God has revealed in its immutable law that one witness is not sufficient but *"at the mouth of two witnesses or at the mouth of three witnesses shall the matter be established"* (Deuteronomy 19:15). *"In the mouth of two or three witnesses shall every word be established"* (II Corinthians 13:1).

Moreover, the NIV perpetuates the big lie that the quotations are from Isaiah the prophet even although in its additional notes it makes clear that one of them is from Malachi. So on its page it carries a direct falsehood.

The saint, with no knowledge of Hebrew or Greek, but knowing the Author of the Book, knows that *"no lie is of the truth"* (I John 2:21). He or she readily separates the precious from the vile, and not following cunningly devised fables, knows that the Authorized Version follows a Greek text most certainly pure when contrasted with that followed or appealed to by the NIV translators. The saint also knows that the texts followed by the NIV translators, however ancient they may be or claim to be, have been seriously and deliberately tampered with by the copyist and purposely changed so that the copyist must have been prompted by some motive in order to make such far-reaching changes in the text, and stands exposed for what he is when he jettisons *"the Prophets"* and blunders so conspicuously. Such a blatant lie inserted into God's Book of Truth is enough for any saint to recognise the counterfeit.

Knowing the attack wielded in the early centuries of Christianity against the essential deity and true, proper and impeccable humanity of our Lord, it can be rightfully concluded that, out of satanic hatred and hellish malice against the truth itself, the intention of the corrupter of God's Holy Word was striking at the central truth of the Word of Salvation and tacitly denying what he dared not openly exclude, that Jesus Christ was *"come in the flesh"*. The saint of God rightly discerns here the *"spirit of antichrist"*.

Surely it must seem strange that the translators of the NIV who profess so loudly their faith in the plenary inspiration of the Holy Word and who, we are informed, had reserves of learning and research, were not alerted against the corruptions of the truth brought into the early Church by the earliest heresies against which the apostles expressly warned.

These heresies, the New Testament expressly and frequently tells us, are the work of *the enemy* seeking to lead men away from the true faith of the Son of God *"who loved us and gave Himself for us,"* the Righteous One for us the unrighteous ones, the Only One True Sacrifice for sins and who by that bloodshedding has brought us to God.

The fact that these NIV translators, out of loyalty to modern scholarship, followed the cunningly devised fables long made manifest in many of the Greek Texts falsely pronounced *pure*, in preference to the consistent text followed by

My plea for *the* Old Sword   81

the Authorized Version translators and not proved impure, demands that we in faithfulness condemn and denounce what they have done.

At the very entrance of their work they have been unable to avoid making our Lord Jesus Christ a stumbling block and thereafter have turned aside in blindness to continue to follow cunningly devised fables and do to the Holy Word of God such things which grieve the Israel of God and make the uncircumcised Philistines rejoice.

This one plain example of contrasting the NIV with the Authorized Version is enough, and the inference follows that it is the duty of the saints of God to see to it that the Authorized Version must be preserved and maintained in preference to, and in rejection of, the NIV.

THE HOLY TRINITY

I John 5:7 *"For there are three that bear record in heaven, the Father, the Word and the Holy Ghost and these three are one."* [Westminster Confession of Faith puts this as a proof text of the doctrine of the Holy Trinity] in Chapter two paragraph III.

The NIV removes verse seven out of their Bible and then subdivides verse eight into verse seven and eight in order to keep the same number of verses in the chapter. According to the NIV translators, those who drew up the great historic confession of the Churches of the Reformation were deceived when they used this text as proof of the Holy Trinity.

Dr Edward Hills, 1912-1981, Presbyterian minister and graduate of Yale University with degrees from Westminster Seminary, Columbia Seminary and Harvard University and a defender of the King James Version, was attacked for defending this great Trinitarian proof text.

> *Ed Hills was treated shamefully. He was ridiculed, blacklisted among fellow scholars (many of whom were unworthy to unlatch the thongs of his sandals). He counted some of his old professors as friends, but William Hendriksen wrote him a sharp letter taking him to task for*

defending I John 5:7 calling it the nadir, the lowest point in textual criticism.

- Letter from Jay Green, March 15, 1995

The Westminster Confession of Faith gives John 1:14 and 18 as proof texts of the doctrine that Christ is the eternally begotten Son of God.

"And the Word was made flesh, and dwelt among us (and we beheld his glory, the glory as of the only begotten of the Father,) full of grace and truth" (John 1:14. Authorized Version).

"No man hath seen God at any time; the only begotten Son, which is in the bosom of the Father, he hath declared him" (John 1:18 Authorized Version).

"The Word became flesh and made his dwelling among us. We have seen his glory, the glory of the One and Only, who came from the Father, full of grace and truth" (John 1:14 NIV).

"No-one has ever seen God, but God the One and Only" (John 1:18 NIV).

The NIV drops "the only begotten Son" completely from these verses.

This puts them into great difficulty and undermines the revelation of the mystery of the Trinity by calling Christ, in verse 18, "the One and only God". What then of the Father and the Holy Ghost?

They certainly err, not knowing the Scriptures.

THE INCARNATION

The Westminster Confession of Faith gives I Timothy 3:16 as a proof text of the Incarnation of the Son.

"And without controversy great is the mystery of godliness: God was manifest in the flesh, justified in the Spirit, seen of angels, preached unto the Gentiles, believed on in the world, received up into glory" (I Timothy 3:16 Authorized Version).

"Beyond all question, the mystery of godliness is great: He appeared in a body, was vindicated by the Spirit, was seen by angels, was preached among the nations, was believed on in the world, was taken up in glory" (I Timothy 3:16 NIV).

Notice the NIV jettisons "God" and substitutes "He", thus following the line of the old Revised Version.

The Authorized Version has no such diluting, undermining, or watering down of the great revealed truths of God in His Holy Word.

The NIV has used small printed footnotes to justify wholesale penknifing of the Word of God. Many of these footnotes, when laid in the balance of truth, are found wanting.

Theodore P Letis, in his recent *A New Hearing for the Authorized Version* (2nd edition page 32) points out:

At Mark 16: 9-20, in the New International Version, there is a footnote stating "The most reliable early manuscripts omit Mark 16:9-20." What they fail to make clear is that out of the approximately 5,487 Greek manuscripts available to scholars, of those that contain Mark, only three manuscripts omit this passage. Two of them, Vaticanus and Sinaiticus, were put to the most detailed study of perhaps any others to date, by Herma Hoskier, in his Codex B and Its Allies: A Study and Indictment (1914). No man in his day, nor perhaps since, knew these two documents as intimately as did Hoskier. The conclusion of his study offered the following consensus:

To receive the Egyptian textual standard [represented by Codices Vaticanus and Sinaiticus] of AD 200-400 is not scientific, and it is certainly not final. The truth is scattered over all our documents and is not inherent entirely in any one document, nor in any two. Hort persuaded himself that where (symbol) B were together... they must be right. This kind of fetishism must be done away with.

Some of the doctrinal changes in the Gospel of Matthew in the NIV listed in The Quarterly Record of the Trinitarian Bible Society are:

Matthew 1:25 omission (om) of "firstborn"; 5:22 om of "without a cause"; 5:44 om) "bless them that curse you etc"; 6:13 om. doxology, 6:18 om. "openly"; 6:27 "hour to his life" for "cubit to his stature"; 9:13, "sinners to repentance" - om. "to repentance"; 11:19 "wisdom proved right by her actions" (A.V. "children", RV. "works")' 12: 47 note "Some Mss. om. verse 47"; 13: 36 "Then he left the crowd" for "sent the multitude away"; 13:36 "Explain to us" for "Declare"; 13:44 om. "again"; 15: 8 om. "This people draweth nigh unto me, etc."; 15:14 om. "of the blind"; 16:8 "having no bread" for "ye have brought no bread"; 17:21 om. whole verse re "prayer and fasting"; 18:11 "om. whole verse "the Son of Man is come to save that which is lost"; 19:16 "Teacher" om. "Good" (A.V. "Good Master"); 19:17 om. "Why do you ask me about what is good?" for "Why callest thou me good?"; 19:17 om. "that is God"; 23:14 om. whole verse; 24:36 "the Father" for "my Father"; 25:13 om. "wherein the Son of man cometh"; 26:28 "blood of the covenant" (om. "new"); 27:35 om. "that it might be fuliflled, etc."

Similar lists could be made of changes in other New Testament Books and the total would certainly not be less than a thousand.

The text omits Acts 8:37 while the note says merely, "Some mss. add verse 37 …" In I Timothy 3:16 "God was manifest in the flesh" is changed to "He appeared in a body," and the clear testimony to the Deity of Christ is lost. In Romans 9:5 another outstanding testimony to the Saviour's Deity is diminished by the footnotes. The text asserts that He is "'God over all," but the notes allow the alternatives, "Christ, who is over all. God be for ever praised!" and "Christ, who is over all. God be for ever praised!"

We can see that even the "super-star" NIV which boasts its orthodoxy and evangelical credentials, and aims by its sales to put the Authorized Version out of business, has laid its destructive tactics against the foundation of Divine Revelation.

We have taken the NIV as an example simply because if they do this evil in the green of the "evangelical" NIV what have they not done in the dry of the whole rash of openly apostate perversions?

"Two new editions of the NIV have appeared in the last three years.

NIV EASY READER'S EDITION

The New International Reader's Version (NIrV) was published by Zondervan in 1994. This is a simplified NIV aimed at a third-grade reading level. Consider the following translation from the NIrV of a key doctrinal passage:

KJV: *"For all have sinned, and come short of the glory of God; Being justified freely by his grace through the redemption that is in Christ Jesus: Whom God hath set forth to be a propitiation through faith in his blood, to declare his righteousness for the remission of sins that are past, through the forbearance of God; To declare, I say, at this time his righteousness: that he might be just, and the justifier of him which believeth in Jesus"* (Romans 3:23-26).

NIrV: *"Everyone has sinned. No one measures up to God's glory. The free gift of God's grace makes all of us right with him. Christ Jesus paid the price to set us free. God gave him as a sacrifice to pay for sins. So he forgives the sins of those who have faith in his blood. God did all of that to prove that he is fair. Because of his mercy he did not punish people for the sins they had committed before Jesus died for them. God did that to prove in our own time that he is fair: he proved that he is right. He also made right with himself those who believe in Jesus."*

By changing the words and the sentence structure, this "easy reader" edition changes the meaning and doctrinal content of the Scriptures.

NIV INCLUSIVE LANGUAGE EDITION

The New International Inclusive Language Edition was published by Hodder and Stoughton in England in 1995, but it was produced by the Committee on Bible Translation (CBT), which is the continuing form of the committee which first completed the NIV in 1978. The inclusive language edition has not yet been published in North America. The British edition of the NIV aims to remove language which fails to make the distinction between men and women that modern western culture requires. "Brethren" is replaced by "brothers and sisters"; "man" is replaced by "humankind" or "people"; etc. Consider a few examples.

Psalm 8: 4
KJV: *"What is man, that thou art mindful of him? and the son of man, that thou visitest him?"*
Inclusive Language NIV: *"What are mere mortals that you are mindful of them, human beings that you care for them?"*

Psalm 34: 20
KJV: *"He keepeth all his bones: not one of them is broken."*
Inclusive Language NIV: *"He protects all their bones, not one of them will be broken."*

This translation corrupts a key prophetic passage. Psalm 34: 20 refers to Christ and the fact that His bones were not broken on the cross. John 19: 32-36 was a direct fulfilment of Psalm 34: 20. The inclusive language NIV changes the singular masculine pronoun "his" to the plural pronoun "their," thereby destroying its prophetic significance.

Luke 17:3
KJV: *"Take heed to yourselves: If thy brother trespass against thee, rebuke him; and if he repent, forgive him."*
Inclusive Language NIV: *"So watch yourselves. Rebuke a brother or sister who sins, and if they repent, forgive them."*

John 66:44
KJV: *"No man can come to me, except the Father which hath sent me draw him: and I will raise him up at the last day."*
Inclusive Language NIV: *"No-one can come to me unless the Father who sent me draws them, and I will raise them up at the last day."*

John 14: 23
KJV: *"Jesus answered and said unto him, If a man love me, he will keep my words: and my Father will love him, and we will come unto him, and make our abode with him."*
Inclusive Language NIV: *"Jesus replied, 'Those who love me will obey my teaching. My Father will love them, and we will come to them and make our home with them."*

This is typical of the incredible perversion of Scripture represented by the inclusive language NIV. The singular pronouns are changed to plural. Christ's sweet and lovely promise to individuals is rendered ineffective by the change to general plural pronouns. Further, "my words" is changed to "my teaching", thus rendering Christ's emphasis on the words of Scripture ineffective by replacing it with the more general idea of teaching.

Revelation 3: 20
KJV: *"Behold, I stand at the door, and knock: if any man hear my voice, and open the door, I will come in to him, and will sup with him, and he with me."*
Inclusive Language NIV: *"Here I am! I stand at the door and knock. If anyone hears my voice and opens the door, I will come in and eat with them, and they with me."*

Again, Christ's tender promise to individuals who receive Him is destroyed by the corrupt inclusive language rendition."

      - David Cloud's most valuable magazine 'O Timothy' Issue 5, 1997

The NIV publishers have now announced they are goint to cease work on the inclusive language editions in the USA and will revise their NIrV publication. We thank God for this victory!

It is a pity they didn't stop publishing the NiV, with its ever changing addtions and subtractions, altogether.

I thank God I have an unchanging Bible in the Authorised Version.

The Authorized Version translators knew from where the attacks were mounted. In their dedication to King James they recorded the advance of the truth giving *"such a blow unto that Man of Sin (the Pope) as will not be healed"*.

They state:

So that if, on the one side, we shall be traduced by Popish Persons at home or abroad, who therefore will malign us, because we are poor instruments to make God's holy Truth to be yet more and more known unto the people, whom they desire still to keep in ignorance and darkness; or if, on the other side, we shall be maligned by self-conceited Brethren, who run their own ways, and give liking unto nothing, but what is framed by themselves, and hammered on their anvil; we may rest secure, supported within by the truth and innocence of a good conscience, having walked the ways of simplicity and integrity, as before the Lord.

Now the Church of Rome would seem at the length to bear a motherly affection towards her children, and to allow them the Scriptures in their mother tongue: but indeed it is a gift, not deserving to be called a gift, an unprofitable gift: they must first get a licence in writing before they may use them; and to get that, they must approve themselves to their Confessor, that is, to be such as are, if not frozen in the dregs, yet soured with the leaven of their superstition. Howbeit, it seemed too much to Clement the eighth that there should be any licence granted to have them in the vulgar tongue, and therefore he over ruleth and frustrateth the grant of Pius the fourth. So much are they afraid of the light of the Scripture, (Lucifugae Scripturarum, as Tertullian speaketh) that they will not trust the people with it, no not as it is set forth by their own sworn men, no not with the licence of their own Bishops and Inquisitors. Yea, so unwilling they are to communicate the Scriptures to the people's understanding in any sort, that they are not ashamed to confess that we forced them to translate it into English against their wills. This seemeth to argue a bad cause, nor a bad conscience, or both. Sure we are, that it is not he that hath good gold, that is afraid to bring it to the touchstone, but he that hath the counterfeit; neither is it the true man that shunneth the light, but the malefactor, lest his deeds should be reproved; neither is it the plain-dealing merchant that is unwilling to have the weights, or the meteyard, brought in place, but he that useth deceit.

The deceits of Popery have so blinded this generation through the chain of ecumenism that even evangelicals are carried away with the dissimilation.

George Sayles Bishop DD, 1836-1914, pastor of the Reformed Church of Orange, New Jersey, exposes the popish poison and doctrinal apostasy which motivated the Revised Version and laid the basis for all the other apostate developments in perverted English translations.

He thundered:

Our modern critics, with arrogance which rises to daring impiety, deny to Christ the insight which they claim for themselves ... The authority of Jesus Christ, God speaking - not from heaven only, but with human lips - has given a sanction to every book and sentence in the Jewish canon, and blasphemy is written on the forehead of any theory which alleges imperfection, error, contradiction or sin in any book in the sacred collection.

- George Sayles Bishop, The Doctrines of Grace and Kindred Themes, p. 93

Consider how painstakingly he examined the question of whether I Timothy 3:16 should read "God":

Soon after 1885 I went to Europe where I spent nearly three weeks in studying this text, I Tim. iii: 16 on the great unicals "C" and "A". Through the kindless of Mr Albert Le Faivre, Minister Plenipotentiary from France to the United States, I had the Codex "C" for one week under my hands to study the membrane with lenses and *under full sunshine. The parchment was also held up by an attendant in front of the great window so that the light could fall through the palimpsest page. I have compared the THEOS of line 14 on folio 119, the one in dispute, with every other THEOS on the page and, out of the five, find it the plainest one there. All five are written with two letters - OY, OY, OC, OY, OΩ. Two of the five only have the line, the mark of contraction, above. Only one of the two, the plainest, is the only one they deny. Three of the five only have the hair mark in the Theta - one of these three is the one they deny. To put it more plainly - the question is, Is it OC "who" or is it OC with a line over the two letters and a mark in the O, God?* **It is beyond question the latter. My eyes are as good as any man's"**

- George Sayles Bishop, "Sheol: The Principle and Tendency of the Revision Examined," The Doctrines of Grace and Kindred Themes, p., 79

I have set before myself a simple straight-forward task - to translate into the language of the common people and in lines of clear, logical light the principles involved in the new version of the Bible and just in what direction it tends. This thing is needed. Nothing at the present time is more needed nor so needed, for I am convinced that the principle at the root of the revision movement has not been fairly understood, not even by many of the revisers themselves, who, charmed by **the siren-like voices addressed to their scholarly feeling***, have yielded themselves to give way, in unconscious unanimous movement, along the wave on which the ship of inspiration floats with easy and accelerating motion, toward rebound, and crash upon the rocks*

- p. 60

That a few changes might be made in both Testaments because of the change of meaning of certain words no changing altering the sense, for the better, no man pretends to deny; but that **all the learned twaddle about "intrinsic and transcriptional probability,"** *"conflation," "neutral texts," "the unique position of B" (The Vatican manuscript) ... that all this theory is false and moonshine and, when applied to God's Word, worse than that; I firmly believe.*

- p. 61

Because I am a minister of Christ ... because my business is to preach and to defend this Book, I cannot and will not keep silence. "If the foundations be destroyed, what can the righteous do?"

- p. 62

THE REVISED VERSION OF THE NEW TESTAMENT IS BASED UPON A NEW, UNCALLED FOR, AND UNSOUND GREEK TEXT - that mainly of Drs Westcott and Hort, which was printed simultaneously with the revision and never before had seen light and which is the most unreliable text perhaps ever printed - one English critic says, "the foulest and most vicious in existence"

- p. 66

I WILL OPPOSE B THE VATICAN MS FIRST, FOREMOST, ALTOGETHER, SIMPLY BECAUSE IT IS THE VATICAN MS, BECAUSE I HAVE TO RECEIVE IT FROM ROME, BECAUSE I WILL HAVE NO BIBLE FROM ROME, NO HELP FROM ROME AND NO COMPLICITY WITH ROME; BECAUSE I BELIEVE ROME TO BE AN APOSTATE. A worshipper of Bread for God; a remover of the sovereign mediatorship of Christ; a destroyer of the true gospel, she teaches a system which, if any man believes or follows as she teaches it, he will infallibly be lost - he must be ... I will not take my Bible - not the bulk of it – from her apostate, foul, deceitful, cruel hands, "Timeo Danaos et dona ferentes" - I fear the Latins bearing presents in their hands.

- p. 69

I have been confirmed in what had before been **A GROWING CONVICTION - THAT THE REVISION MOVEMENT, DATING FROM THE FINDING OF TISCHENDORF'S** *[Aleph], unconsciously to most, but consciously to the Unitarian - to the Messrs Vance Smith, Robertson Smith, etc. - liberal members of the New Testament Company, was* **RUNNING STEADILY IN ONE DIRECTION THROUGH THREE POINTS: FIRST TO WEAKEN AND DESTROY THE BINDING FORCE OF INSPIRATION IN THE VERY WORDS.** *Second, To weaken and destroy the five Points of Grace founded on "Free Will a Slave". Third, To weaken and destroy the old-fashioned notion of Hell as a place and a state of immediate, everlasting and utterly indescribable torment into which impenitent men go at once the moment they die.*

- p. 74

The Revised Version weakens and removes the deity of Christ in many places - one I mention in particular I Timothy 3:16, "Great is the mystery of godliness, God was manifest in the flesh". The Revised Version [as do all modern versions] leaves out Theos, God ... Dr Scrivener, the foremost English critic, says it is Theos ... That conviction of Dr Scrivener is my conviction and on the very same grounds - **A CONVICTION SO DEEP THAT I WILL NEVER YIELD IT, NOR ADMIT AS A TEXT OF MY FAITH A BOOK PRETENDING TO BE A REVELATION FROM GOD WHICH LEAVES THAT WORD OUT. THE HOLY GHOST HAS WRITTEN IT - LET NO MAN DARE TOUCH IT - GREAT IS THE MYSTERY OF GODLINESS, GOD WAS MANIFEST IN THE FLESH.**

- (pp. 78-80).

LET ME SAY CLEARLY AND PLAINLY THAT THE DOCTRINE OF THE AUTHORIZED VERSION (KJV) OF THE ENGLISH BIBLE IS UNSURPASSABLY PRE-EMINENT BEING COUCHED IN SOUND WORDS IN KEEPING WITH UNWAVERING BELIEF IN THE REVEALED TRUTHS OF THE WORD OF GOD.

8. The reverence of the English Authorised Version (KJV) of the Holy Bible is unsurpassably pre-eminent

casting the hem of its holy garment over every sentence, word and syllable

The Holy Bible means Holy Book. The Authorized Version breathes the reverence of the Holy Bible of which it is the translation.

Just the same way as the Church of Rome attacked the translation of the Scripture into what was called the VulgarTongue (i.e. the mother tongue of the particular country) so today there has been a resurrection of that antagonism by those who have adopted the Romish principle, but applied to a different set of circumstances. They simply rehearse the old Roman argument that no translation can be truly the Word of God.

Deluded spokesmen say with so-called superior and scholarly airs, "What is the use of insisting on any special doctrine of inspiration when you know it cannot apply to our English version? The original Hebrew and Greek may have been inspired but you do not surely claim inspiration for a mere translation?"

Dr Hugh Martin, that mighty theologian of Scotland in the last century, ably answered that question thus:-

"It would thus appear that inspiration is conceived of as some spiritual dye or colour or flavour which is washed out or

evaporates in the use of translation, and that however good and satisfactory the translation may be. For it is not any hypothetical insufficiency, erroneousness, or general badness of the translation to which this melancholy result is supposed to be assignable, but to translation generally. But this is just a misapprehension, or a refusal to accept in its plain and simple meaning the great truth that the Scriptures are the Word of God - God's Word committed to writing by Himself. For just try the idea in relation to any other book and its authorship. Here we shall say, is "Newton's Principia". It was originally in Latin."

"This, let us say, is an English version. Is it not Newton's Principia? Is the authorship of it gone in the process of translation? That is the point. Is the written Word of God no longer God's written Word, because it has been translated into English?"

"Holy men of old, as they were moved and guided by the inspiration of the Holy Ghost, wrote, each of them respectively, what God decreed they should write as their contributions to a volume which He intended to be His own written Word and published works - His wondrous gift to the sons of men. The good Spirit of God is too abounding in His goodness to have written on His volume, churlishly, the formula, "Rights of translation reserved". And the same all-wise Spirit of God is too abundant in wisdom and too sparing of miracle to have undertaken its translation into all languages (or any) Himself. But a great part of His Scripture being non-miraculously translated ere the volume was completed, the Spirit of the Lord, infinitely far from the character alike of churl and of pedant and not despising the translation because not divinely perfect - stamping with His approbation for ever the principle that the translated Word of God is still the Word of God when translated, and takes rank with yet untranslated Scripture, scrupled not freely to quote, and to wield as still possessing divine character and authority, what the Seventy of Alexandra had written in Greek translation of the Hebrew Scriptures. And if He being, in His graciousness, not ill to please, but pleased with reverential honest effort - counts translated Scripture God's Scripture still, we, surely may be content."

- Inspiration of Scripture p 20

Westminster Confession of Faith chapter 1 paragraph VIII:-

"The Old Testament in Hebrew (which was the native language of the people of God of old), and the New Testament in Greek (which at the time of the writing of its was most generally known to the nations), being immediately inspired by God, and by his singular care and providence kept pure in all ages, are therefore authentical, so as in all controversies of religion, the Church is finally to appeal unto them. But because these original tongues are not known to all the people of God, who have right unto and interest in the scriptures, and are commanded, in the fear of God, to read and search them, therefore they are to be translated into the vulgar language of every nation unto which they come, that the Word of God dwelling plentifully in all, they may worship Him in acceptable manner, and through patience and comfort of the scriptures, may have hope."

The reverence of the original Scripture has been wonderfully preserved in the Authorized Version translation. There is a sacredness, a reverence, and a spiritual uniqueness about the sentences, the words and the syllables which make them unsurpassably pre-eminent above all the other English translations.

It is this holy anointing oil of sacredness which, like Aaron's anointing, runs to the hem of the garment and so includes the whole. This sacredness and holy awe produced and produces the spiritual influence of the Old Book in the lives of the people.

Should it be surprising that this Ancient Book made known to each succeeding generation of English people should have such an influence?

As Dr McAfee has said:

It is the one great piece of English literature which is universal property. Since the day it was published it has been kept available for everybody. No other book has ever had its chance. English-speaking people have always been essentially religious. They have always had a profound regard for the terms, the institutions, the purposes of religion. Partly that has been maintained by the Bible; but the Bible in its turn has been maintained by it. So it has come about that English-speaking people, though they have many books, are essentially people of one Book. Wherever they are, the Bible is. Queen Victoria has it nearby when the messenger from the Orient appears, and lays her hand upon it to say that it is the foundation of the prosperity of England. But the poor housewife in the cottage, with only a crust for food, stays her soul with it. The Puritan creeps into hiding with the Book. The settler may have his Shakespeare; he will surely have his Bible. As the long wagon-train creeps across the plain to seek the Western shore, there may be no other book in all the train; but the Bible will be there. Find any settlement of men who speak the English tongue, wherever they make their home, and the Bible is among them. When did any book have such a chance to influence men? It is the one undisturbed heritage of all who speak the English tongue. It binds the daughter and the mother-country together, and gathers into the same bond the scattered remnants of the English-speaking race the world around. Its language is the one speech they all understand. Strange it would be if it had not a profound influence upon history!"*

- pp 198-199

The very expression in speech of the truths of the Bible in the Authorized Version carry with them their own intrinsic power and godliness. Their form of sound words is the touchstone which has tried the spirits of English speaking men and women no matter how different they may be in colour, class, creed, country and time.

Dr McAfee continues:

"The influence of the English Bible on English-speaking history for the last three hundred years is only the influence of its fundamental truths. It has moved with tremendous impact on the wills of men. It has made the great human ideas clear and definite; it has made them beautiful and attractive; but that has not been enough. It has

reached also the springs of action. It has given men a sense of need and also a sense of strength, a sense of outrage and a sense of power to correct the wrong. There it has differed from most books. Frederick Robertson said that he read only books with iron in them, and, as he read, their atoms of iron entered the blood, and it ran more red for them. There is iron in this Book, and it has entered the blood of the human race. Where it has entered most freely, the red has deepened; and nowhere has it deepened more than in our English-speaking races. The iron of our blood is from this King James version."

-pp 202-203

There are four great spiritual movements which colour the last four centruies - The Quakers, The Puritans, The Methodists and The Evangelicals.

All these movements had an immense influence in moulding and shaping the passing of these centuries.

Many arguments might be ignited about Fox, about Owen, and the Puritans, about Whitefield and the Wesley brothers and about Spurgeon, the Second Evangelical Awakening and the birth of Modern Missions.

There is no argument, no dispute and no doubt that all these movements issued from the Bible and led the peoples involved back to the English Authorized Version.

There is but one statue the English designed should stand under the shadow of its Parliament House walls. That statue is not one of England's many kings and queens. You will search in vain for them., That statue is of a plain man, a rugged fighting man, a martyred man, a man whose body, just three years   buried, was unearthed by sycophants' hands, hanged on the Tyburn hanging tree for a day, beheaded, its trunk thown into a pit and the head fixed to a spike at Parliament House. Who is that man? It is Oliver Cromwell. The Book that made that man's blood run red, aye ruby red, was the English Bible. The sacredness of reverence of this Book had brought him from his Egypt of sin to the redemption of Golgotha's Lamb, and like another Moses he led our nation to the promised land of liberty.

There is no doubt about it, the reverent language of the Authorized Version produced reverent language on the lips of those whose hearts had been changed to a heart of godly reverence from a heart of ungodly irreverence.

There is a reverence in the Authorized Version's description of the sex act which causes no blushes to either young or old. The Authorized Version adopted the expression "knew and conceived". Contrast that, the chaste language, to the language of many of the modern versions.

Compare Saul's attack on his son Jonathan in I Samuel 20:30 as it was first translated in *The Living Bible*, (so-called) *"You son of a bitch"* to the Authorized Version's *"Son of the perverse rebellious woman"*, which by the way is admitted in the most recent edition of the Living Bible as the literal rendering.

Further, compare the Living Bible's translation of Elijah's mocking of the prophets of Baal in I Kings 18:27 *"else he is out sitting on the toilet"* (this is both inaccurate and ugly) to the Authorized Version's *"he is pursuing"*. Moreover, it is what the original Hebrew says.

The reverence of the Authorized Version is also demonstrated in its use of *Thee* and *Thou*.

The use of *Thee* and *Thou* especially in reference to Deity has about it a peculiar reverence and awe most needed in this irreverent age.

Some modern versions not only depart from the consistency of the Authorized Version in using these pronouns of both God and man. Satanically they make a distinction in Scriptures concerning Christ in order to strike at His Deity.

For a case in point take the New English Bible:

The Authorized Version universally uses "Thee" and "Thou" whether these pronouns are used of God or of man. If the translators of the New English Bible are going to be consistent they would use "You" and "Yours" all through their translation. For some reason they have retained "thee" and "'thou" in the passages where God is referred to, and "you" and "yours" elsewhere. For example, in the book of the Revelation chapter 11:17 God is addressed in the New

English Bible thus: "We give thee thanks, O Lord God, sovereign over all, who art and who wast, because thou hast taken thy great power into thy hands and entered upon thy reign." Notice the pronoun "thou" used here concerning Deity. Never however, in the Gospels in the New English Bible is "thee" or "thou" used of our Lord Jesus Christ. They consistently reject the Deity of the Son of God. For example, in Matthew 16:16 the great Confession of Peter in Caesarea-Philippi is changed to read: "You are the Messiah". Here again Christ to the New English Bible translators is just a man. This distinction of pronouns is unwarranted and is a subtle act to separate Jesus Christ from God, an act which is in entire contradiction of the Scriptures.

Dr Mikre-Sellassie, a translation consultant of the United Bible Societies states in *The Bible Translation* April, 1988:

> *Translators, and especially those in common language projects, may find it strange and surprising to hear a consultant recommending use of the King James Version for translation ... The archaic English pronouns of the King James Version distinguish number in the second person pronoun in all cases, as shown in the accompanying table. Thus the King James Version can certainly render an important service to those translators who do not have any knowledge of the source languages of the Bible and therefore work only from an English base, in easily distinguishing between "you singular" and "you plural".*

	SINGULAR			PLURAL
1st Person	I			we
2nd Person	thou/thee/thy/thine			ye/ you/your
	Masculine	Feminine	Neuter	
3rd Person	he	she	it	they

Hence it is impossible to communicate this important grammatical point without Elizabethan Biblical English terms as used in the Authorised version.

The pronoun "you" started to be used instead of "Thou" towards the end of the 13th century, and this use extended in the following three centuries. But the translators of the Authorised Version did not conform to this rising usage, so that, when the Authorised Version appeared, it was not in some ways in the usage of the 17th century. Why did the Authorised Version's translators not adopt the up-to-date English of their time? For one particular reason which many people have perhaps not realised accuracy of translation! Whenever the Hebrew and Greek texts use the singular of the pronoun, so does the Authorised Version; and whenever these texts use the plural, so does the Authorised Version. In other words, the Authorised Version translators stuck closely to the Biblical usage, and translated the Word of God using a kind of Biblical style of English. The version was a faithful one above all else. The same cannot be said so completely for any other English Bible. In fact most are nowhere near that standard. There is a distinct loss of accuracy in translation if "You" is used for the singular as well as the plural: it becomes an ambiguous word. The Authorised Version informs us correctly on what was the proper original sense. Thus, in Luke 22:31, 32, the Lord says to Peter, "Satan hath desired to have you, that he may sift you as wheat," "you" here referring to Peter and the other disciples; "But I have prayed for thee, that thy faith fail not," "thee" and "thy" referring to Peter only. Such shades of meaning are completely lost when "you" is used throughout.

- "The Old is Better" by Alfred Lesell

THERE IS NO DOUBT ABOUT IT, THE REVERENCE OF THE ENGLISH AUTHORISED VERSION (KJV) OF THE HOLY BIBLE IS UNSURPASSABLY PRE-EMINENT OVER EVERY SENTENCE, WORD AND SYLLABLE.

9 The history of the English Authorised Version (KJV) of the Holy Bible is unsurpassably pre-eminent,

having preserved for centuries the Word of God for the English speaking peoples of the whole world, and those evangelised by them.

When, after His baptism by John and just before the commencement of His public ministry, our Lord Jesus Christ met the greatest foeman of God's Word - the Devil. His words were, *'It is written, man shall not live by bread alone but by every word which proceedeth out of the mouth of God'.* Matthew 4:4.

These are Christ's first recorded words to Satan, that old serpent the Devil, the would-be destroyer of the Holy Scriptures.

The faith of the Son of God concerning the Word of God is set forth here in the greatest brevity but with the greatest clarity.

Someone wrote a book once in defence of the Holy Scripture and entitled it, *'Revelation plus Inspiration equals the Bible.'*

The writer, however, sadly missed something. What was that something which he missed?

Look carefully at our Saviour's Confession of Faith on the Holy Scripture.

There are three things here, not just two.

One, there is **Divine Revelation** - *'proceedeth out of the mouth of God.'*

Two, there is **Divine Inspiration** - *'man cannot live by bread alone but by every word of God.'* See Luke 4:4.

Three, there is **Divine Preservation** - *'It is written.'*

Note, Christ used the perfect tense which, according to Greek scholars, states a finalised action with a continuous state of being.

The Lord was saying, *'It was written, It is written and it will be forever written.'* So it is Divine Revelation plus Divine Inspiration plus Divine Preservation equals the Divine Bible.

These all, without exception, cover the whole field of every Word of God.

There is no such thing as verbal Revelation without verbal Inspiration and there is no such thing as verbal Inspiration without verbal Preservation. In all cases it is not partial but plenary i.e. full, complete, perfect.

We should note carefully that the plenary Inspiration which enabled the writers of Holy Scripture to record accurately every word spoken in plenary Revelation and thus produced the Original Scriptures, does not apply to the translation of the Scriptures.

This new doctrine called Dual Inspiration which affirms that the process extends to the Authorised Version is known as Ruckmanism, after Dr. Peter Ruckman who popularised this doctrine, had its beginnings in Rome. Rome officially exalted the Latin Version, the Vulgate, into a place of eminence above the Originals. No translation can take the place of the Original autographs of Scripture. The plenary Preservation of Scripture is in no way to be confused with this false doctrine of so-called dual inspiration. True copies of original autographs of Holy Scripture cannot be altered in any way or expanded by any translation. The Canon of Scripture is closed.

The Divine Revelation, put into writing the verbally Infallible Scriptures though Divine Inspiration, must have Divine Preservation in order to be available to all generations.

The verbal Inspiration of the Scriptures demands the verbal Preservation of the Scriptures.

Those who would deny the need for verbal Preservation cannot be accepted as being really committed to verbal Inspiration. If there is no preserved Word of God today then the work of Divine Revelation and Divine Inspiration has perished.

In such a case any Bible is as good as any other. Hence the multiplication and continuing changes of perverted English versions of the Bible on the market today.

Those who only believe in a partial preservation are not much better. To say that God has preserved most of the Original Scriptures but not them all, robs us of every Word of God. Therefore we cannot live. This is but another way to pen-knife God's every Word.

Those who do not believe that God preserved His Word are really going down the path of final rejection of that Book of which the Lord Jesus Christ said, *"The Word of God cannot be broken."*

Thank God, no potency can disintegrate this Rock.

The testimony of Scripture to this Divinely Revealed Doctrine is clear and plain. Ponder these Scriptures.

> Psalm 78: 1-7: *'Give ear, O my people, to my law: incline your ears to the words of my mouth. I will open my mouth in a parable: I will utter dark sayings of old. Which we have heard and known, and our fathers have told us. We will not hide them from their children, shewing to the generation to come the praises of the* LORD *and his strength, and his wonderful works that he hath done. For he*

established a testimony in Jacob, and appointed a law in Israel, which he commanded our fathers, that they should make them known to their children: that the generation to come might know them, even the children which should be born; who should arise and declare them to their children: That they might set their hope in God, and not forget the works of God, but keep his commandments.'

Psalm 105: 8: 'He hath remembered his covenant for ever, the word which he commanded to a thousand generations.'

Psalm 119: 160: 'Thy word is true from the beginning: and every one of thy righteous judgments endureth for ever.'

Ecclesiastes 3: 14: 'I know that, whatsoever God doeth, it shall be for ever: nothing can be put to it, nor any thing taken from it: and God doeth it, that men should fear before him.'

Matthew 4: 4: 'But he answered and said, It is written, Man shall not live by bread alone, but by every word that proceedeth out of the mouth of God.'

Luke 4: 4: 'And Jesus answered him, saying, It is written, That man shall not live by bread alone, but by every word of God.'

Matthew 5: 17-18: 'Think not that I am come to destroy the law, or the prophets: I am not come to destroy, but to fulfil.'

Matthew 24: 35: 'Heaven and earth shall pass away, but my words shall not pass away.'

I Peter 1: 23-25: 'Being born again, not of corruptible seed, but of incorruptible, by the word of God, which liveth and abideth for ever. For all flesh is as grass, and all the glory of man as the flower of grass. The grass withereth, and the flower thereof falleth away: But the word of the Lord endureth forever. And this is the word which by the gospel is preached unto you.'

John 12: 48: 'He that rejecteth me, and receiveth not my words, hath one that judgeth him: the word that I have spoken, the same shall judge him in the last day.'

John 17: 8: "For I have given unto them the words which thou gavest me; and they have received them, and have known surely that I came out from thee, and they have believed that thou didst send me."

Commenting on these two last verses. Dr. Thomas M. Strouse in his valuable booklet, *'Fundamentalism and the Authorised Version'* published by Tabernacle Baptist Theological Seminary, Virginia Beach, VA 23464, USA states:

"In reference to John 12: 48, Christ has said, "The word that I have spoken, the same shall judge him in the last day." The expression 'the word' translates *ho logos* and it refers to the totality of Christ's canonical and inscripturated words. One must expect that Christ's canonical and inscripturated words will be the ever-present standard by which all mankind will be judged.

The latter verse, John 17: 8, states, "For I have given unto them the words which thou gavest me; and they have received them, and have known surely that I came out from thee, and they have believed that thou didst send me." The verse teaches that Christ's responsibility before the Father is to give His believers the Father's words (remata). Several questions must be answered. What and where are these words? Has Christ fulfilled His responsibility in preserving the Father's words to His immediate audience and to future generations (cf. v. 20)? The answer to the first question is that the Father's words are the canonical Scriptures. The second question must be answered in the affirmative. The Lord Jesus Christ has the power, character and means to preserve the Scriptures. Not only has the Lord preserved His Word to His immediate audience, but He has preserved it through their word (*logou*, e.g. the NT Scripture) for future generations.

This passage also teaches the Christian's responsibility towards Christ's preserved words of the Father. Christ states that believers 'have received them". The word 'received' translates *elabon* which is a 3rd person, plural, 2nd aorist, indicative, active verb from *lambano* and it means 'take' or 'receive'. The believer's responsibility is not to restore the 4th century text (i.e. Westcott and Hort) through the science of textual criticism (advocates of modern versions), but to receive the providentally preserved words of Christ. When the doctrine of Providential Preservation is rejected or ignored, all that is left is man's imperfect and rationalistic efforts. Biblically, Christians have had the expectation from this passage to receive the providentially preserved words from the Father, through Christ, through the *autographs* of the apostles. Believers of the 17th century confirmed their belief in receiving the providentially preserved Scripture by naming the common Greek text the *textum ... nunc ab omnibus receptum* ('the text now received by all').

- pp 8 and 9

Surely here we have the Doctrine of Divine Preservation divinely revealed. The preserved Scriptures cannot be lost or caused in any way to perish. As of the God who uttered them, so we can say, 'Thou remainest!'

It is interesting to note that the new Bibles vary the words of Psalm 12: 6-7 and so eliminate the testimony of that verse to the Divine Preservation of the Scriptures. They insist that the 'them' of verse seven is not a reference to God's words but to God's people. So they change the 'him' singular of verse 5 into 'them' plural of verse 7 and destroy the text's testimony to the Preservation of God's Word.

God's providential preservation of His own Word ensured that the true Scriptures were not hidden away in the library of the Antichrist nor in a monastery of 'Greek Catholic' idolatry at the time when Tyndale prepared his Bible. Faithful and true copies of the originals were at hand for the Divine Bombshell (Tyndale's translation of God's Holy Word into English) which would smash the Roman Antichrist. He translated into English the Preserved Word of God, not the Perverted Word of God.

A return to the Apostolic Gospel comes as a result of Tyndale's work. A return to the Apostate Gospel comes as a result of the translation of Rome's long-hidden, perverted text and other such perverted texts in the Modern Perversions of the Scriptures.

The Authorised Version translated into English the Preserved Word of God and so preserved for the English speaking peoples of the World, the Word of the Living God, the only infallible Rule of Faith and Practice.

From 1611 until 1881 it preserved the Word of God to the English speaking peoples of the 17th, 18th and 19th centuries. To them it became the one true Bible in English.

Herein lay the strength of the advancement of the Historic Christian Faith. One Bible was the last court of appeal in all matters of belief and behaviour.

When Satan couldn't destroy the Bible by fire and sword he adopted the plan to duplicate the Bible, and the AV Bible had another placed alongside it, the Revision Version of 1881. The battle of the Bibles commenced and has raged ever since. As English speaking people were directed away from the true Word of God the declension of the Gospel faith took place, paving the way for the end time apostasy of our day. Now we have increasing New English Bibles and increasing changing Bibles. The anchor is gone and the storms tear our frail barques with their destructive teeth.

From the 17th century and into the 20th century the AV preserved the Word of God not only for the English speaking peoples but for all those whom they evangelised. The AV became the Bible of those nations brought to Christ through the great Christian Missionary crusade of almost four centuries.

All those evangelised, both at home and abroad, were able to come to the same conclusion as the great Professor Gaussen:

"that not only was the Scripture inspired when it was written but that this Word is now in our possession ... and holding the sacred text in our hand ... we can explain with gratitude, I now hold in my hands the Eternal Word of God."

THE HISTORY OF THE AUTHORISED VERSION (KJV) OF THE ENGLISH BIBLE IS UNSURPASSABLY PRE-EMINENT, HAVING PRESERVED FOR CENTURIES THE WORD OF GOD FOR THE ENGLISH SPEAKING PEOPLES OF THE WORLD AND THOSE EVANGELISED BY THEM.

10 The fruits of the English Authorised Version (KJV) of the Holy Bible are unsurpassably pre-eminent,

being so mighty and so manifold that there is not room enough to receive them

The fruits of the Authorised Version are inexhaustible in their spiritual fruitfulness. That fruitfulness can never be chronicled. There is not room enough to receive it, let alone record it.

In his thrilling book, *The Bible Stands Up To Life,* Thomas Tiplady in his preface has this to say:

> "Many years ago a traveller found a Kaffir boy playing at marbles with a stone which looked very ordinary, until he took it in his hand and carefully examined it. After examination he declared the stone to be a diamond, and under the ground where the Kaffir boy played there are now the famous Kimberley mines. For centuries men had walked over Kimberley's dusty surface without suspecting their nearness to mines of wealth beyond the dreams of avarice. In like manner Europe, for ages, had in its midst a book of truth and beauty unequalled in literature, but to the mass of men it was a closed mine. Its discovery and reopening caused an infinitely greater sensation than the opening of the Kimberley mines, and has enriched all nations."

It has been well said, "There are some things too mysterious for man to define and too profound for him to measure and that is this Bible - the Book of the Only Wise God."

The Bible is the Book of God's power. It made Luther a new man and the monk who shook the world. Like a bolt of heavenly thunder, with the Torch of Scripture he set the whole world on fire.

What a conflagration it kindled! God's Word is FIRE! The power of the Word of God breathes resurrection into the valley of dry bones. Decaying eras suddenly became epochs of Life, Life, Abundant Life.

What a change it made to England. John Richard Green in his history classic, *The History of the English Speaking People* states:

"No greater moral change ever passed over a nation than passed over England during the years which parted the middle of the reign of Elizabeth from the meeting of the Long Parliament. England became the people of a book, and that book was the Bible. It was as yet the one English book which was familiar to every Englishman: it was read at churches and read at home, and everywhere its words, as they fell on ears which custom had not deadened to their force and beauty, kindled a startling enthusiasm.

But far greater than its effect on literature or social phrase was the effect of the Bible on the character of the people at large. Elizabeth might silence or tune the pulpits; but it was impossible for her to silence or tune the great preachers of justice and mercy, and truth, who spoke from the book which she had again opened for her people. The whole moral effect which is produced nowadays by the religious newspaper, the tract, the essay, the lecture, the missionary report, the sermon, was then produced by the Bible alone. And its effect in this way, however dispassionately we examine it, was simply amazing. The whole temper of the nation was changed."

But what was accomplished in Elizabeth's day in England, has been accomplished throughout the whole world wherever the Authorised Version of the Holy

Bible has been carried, circulated and proclaimed by the English speaking peoples.

Time would fail to tell of the triumphs of the Holy Word as it burned its way around the whole world, delivering souls with its light and destroying sin with its flame.

What a great matter this little fire has kindled!

The vision of the little book in Christ's hand in Revelation chapter 10 tells the story in grand apocalyptic language.

> "And I saw another mighty angel come down from heaven, clothed with a cloud: and a rainbow was upon his head, and his face was as it were the sun, and his feet as pillars of fire. And he had in his hand a little book open: and he set his right foot upon the sea, and his left foot on the earth, And cried with a loud voice, as when a lion roareth: and when he had cried, seven thunders uttered their voices. And when the seven thunders had uttered their voices, I was about to write: and I heard a voice from heaven saying unto me, Seal up those things which the seven thunders uttered, and write them not. And the angel which I saw stand upon the sea and upon the earth lifted up his hand to heaven, And sware by him that liveth for ever and ever, who created heaven and the things that therein are, and the earth, and the things that therein are, and the sea, and the things which are therein, that there should be time no longer: But in the days of the voice of the seventh angel, when he shall begin to sound, the mystery of God should be finished, as he hath declared to his servants the prophets. And the voice which I heard from heaven spake unto me again, and said, Go and take the little book which is open in the hand of the angel which standeth upon the sea and upon the earth. And I went unto the angel, and said unto him, Give me the little book. And he said unto me, Take it, and eat it up: and it shall make thy belly bitter, but it shall be in they mouth sweet as honey. And I took the little book out of the angel's hand, and ate it up; and it was in my mouth sweet as honey: and as soon as I had eaten it, my belly was bitter. And he said unto me, Thou must prophesy again before many peoples, and nations, and tongues, and kings."

Abraham Lincoln said a year before his martyrdom:

"I am profitably engaged in reading the Bible. Take all this Book upon reason that you can and the balance upon faith and you will live and die a better man."

That Bible of Abraham Lincoln's was the Authorised Version (KJV).

John Wesley meditated:

"I have thought, I am a creature of a day, passing through life as an arrow through the air. I am a spirit come from God and returning to God: just hovering over the great gulf; till, a few moments hence, I am no more seen; I drop into an unchanging eternity! I want to know one thing - the way to heaven: how to land safe on that happy shore. God Himself has condescended to teach the way: for this very end He came from heaven. He hath written it down in a Book. O give me that Book! At any price, give me the Book of God!"

That book of John Wesley's was the Authorised Version (KJV).

YES, THE FRUITS OF THE ENGLISH AUTHORISED VERSION (KJV) OF THE HOLY BIBLE ARE UNSURPASSABLY PRE-EMINENT, BEING SO MIGHTY AND SO MANIFOLD THAT THERE IS NOT ROOM ENOUGH TO RECEIVE THEM.

"Wherefore lay apart all filthiness and superfluity of naughtiness, and receive with meekness the engrafted word, which is able to save your souls. But be ye doers of the word, and not hearers only, deceiving your own selves. For if any be a hearer of the word, and not a doer, he is like unto a man beholding his natural face in a glass: For he beholdeth himself, and goeth his way, and straightway forgetteth what manner of man he was. But whoso looketh into the perfect law of liberty, and continueth therein, he being not a forgetful hearer, but a doer of the work, this man shall be blessed in his deed."

- James 1: 21-25

THE
IAN R. K. PAISLEY LIBRARY

OTHER BOOKS IN THIS SPECIAL SERIES

♦ **Christian Foundations**

♦ **An Exposition of the Epistle to the Romans**

♦ **The Garments of Christ**

♦ **Sermons on Special Occasions**

♦ **Expository Sermons**

♦ **A Text a Day keeps the Devil Away**

♦ **The Rent Veils at Calvary**

AVAILABLE FROM

AMBASSADOR PRODUCTIONS, LTD.

Providence House
16 Hillview Avenue,
Belfast, BT5 6JR
Telephone: 01232 658462

Emerald House
1 Chick Springs Road, Suite 102
Greenville, South Carolina, 29609
Telephone: 1 800 209 8570